CYRUS FIELD'S BIG DREAM

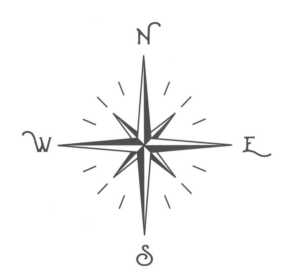

CYRUS FIELD'S

BIG DREAM

The Daring Effort to Lay the First Transatlantic Telegraph Cable

by Mary Morton Cowan

CALKINS CREEK
AN IMPRINT OF HIGHLIGHTS
Honesdale, Pennsylvania

Calkins Creek
An Imprint of Highlights
815 Church Street
Honesdale, Pennsylvania 18431

Printed in China

ISBN: 978-1-62979-556-0 (hc) · 978-1-68437-142-6 (eBook)

Library of Congress Control Number: 2018933313

First edition

10 9 8 7 6 5 4 3 2 1

Designed by William D. Mack

Titles and quotes set in Burford

Chapter numbers and drop caps set in Haymaker

Text set in Geogrotesque Slab

Captions set in Brother 1816

FOR CATHERINE, DAVID, TIMOTHY, AND MARIANNE, WHO MAINTAIN A WONDERFUL CONNECTION WITH ME, USING TODAY'S METHODS OF "INSTANT" COMMUNICATION

~ CYRUS WEST FIELD ~

CONTENTS

CHAPTER 1   **A WILD IDEA** 8

CHAPTER 2   **A COUNTRY BOY** 12

CHAPTER 3   **THE BIG CITY** 20

CHAPTER 4   **RAGS TO RICHES** 30

CHAPTER 5   **MOUNTAIN ADVENTURE** 42

CHAPTER 6   **A TELEGRAPH COMPANY** 52

CHAPTER 7   **NEWFOUNDLAND** 62

CHAPTER 8   **CROSSING THE ATLANTIC** 74

CHAPTER 9   **TRY AGAIN** 94

CHAPTER 10   **"CYRUS THE GREAT"** 110

CHAPTER 11   **"HUMBUG"** 126

CHAPTER 12   **WAR** 136

CHAPTER 13   **"THE WONDER OF THE SEAS"** 150

CHAPTER 14   **"THE CABLE IS LAID"** 168

Epilogue 185

Author's Note 188

Timeline 191

Connections to Make 196

Acknowledgments 198

Source Notes 200

Selected Bibliography 209

Index 213

Picture Credits 224

"BOLD CYRUS FIELD HE SAID, SAYS HE,

I HAVE A PRETTY NOTION

THAT I CAN RUN A TELEGRAPH

ACROSS THE ATLANTIC OCEAN."

FROM THE POEM "HOW CYRUS LAID THE CABLE"
BY JOHN GODFREY SAXE

A WILD IDEA

(1854)

One cold winter night in 1854, two men climbed the steps to Cyrus Field's house in New York City. One was Cyrus's older brother Matthew, the other an Englishman named Frederic Gisborne. A servant ushered them in to Cyrus's library. Fire crackled in the fireplace.

Matthew had met Mr. Gisborne in the lobby of the Astor House hotel in January. Gisborne had a dilemma with a telegraph project in Newfoundland, and Matthew thought Cyrus could help. At age thirty-four, Cyrus had recently retired, after making a fortune as a paper merchant. Now he was searching for new ways to invest his time and money. He wasn't particularly interested in Newfoundland, but he gave in to his brother's pestering and agreed to talk with Mr. Gisborne.

Cyrus didn't know how telegraphs worked. He knew only that wires were strung on poles, and messages traveled through them instantly—and he clearly understood the value of instant communication. Many companies were conducting business by telegraph over North America's expanding network of wires. Lines already connected Nova Scotia and New Brunswick in the Province of Canada to Maine, south to New York City, and farther down the Atlantic coast.

Matthew Field brought Frederic Gisborne here to Cyrus's home in New York City's wealthy Gramercy Park neighborhood to talk about a telegraph project.

Mr. Gisborne told Cyrus he wanted to connect the island of Newfoundland with the mainland by telegraph.

Cyrus wondered why.

Gisborne explained that messages from Europe could reach the United States faster if ships could drop letters off at St. John's, the island's easternmost port, and send them as telegrams to New York and other cities. Messages would whiz through wires and arrive in New York two or three days before ships could deliver them.

Gisborne unrolled a map and spread it out on the library table. He explained to Cyrus that the Newfoundland legislature had granted his company permission to build and operate a telegraph line across the island—all the way from the east coast to the southwest corner. An underwater cable to the mainland would complete the connection.

But Gisborne had a problem.

Crews had strung only forty miles of line when he ran out of money. He couldn't pay his workers. His New York financiers backed out, and he was arrested for not paying his debts.

Cyrus knew Gisborne had come to him in search of money. He wanted to know how much Gisborne needed.

Fifty thousand dollars to pay his debts, Gisborne said, plus money for his company to finish stringing the line.

Cyrus stood by the table, calculating dollars in his head. *Why pay a man's debt and invest in a bankrupt company to lay a telegraph line across the Newfoundland wilderness? All to save two or three days' travel time to communicate with Europe?* No. Cyrus was a shrewd businessman, and this sounded like a waste of his money. He made no promises to Gisborne.

After their meeting, Cyrus couldn't stop thinking. About telegraphs. About instant communication. And about trade. London was the center of world trade. Cyrus knew how frustrating it was to wait weeks when trading with British companies. It took ten or more days for ships to deliver mail, and ten more for a reply—*if* the ships didn't go down at sea.

Restless, Cyrus spun his library globe. That's when he noticed Newfoundland was much closer to England than he had thought. Why not lay a telegraph cable all the way across the ocean? Messages would arrive in minutes. People could be in touch every day instead of waiting nearly a month for letters to be shipped back and forth.

What a wild idea! With the persistence Cyrus had shown since boyhood, he latched onto his idea, determined to make it work. And that changed everything.

"CYRUS WAS THE 'SQUIRMIEST'
CHILD THEY HAD EVER SEEN."

SAMUEL CARTER III

A COUNTRY BOY

(1819–1835)

Cyrus West Field liked to explore the valley of the Housatonic River with his brothers. He was never physically strong like they were, but he was determined to keep up. They rode horseback across meadows. They hiked through wooded hillsides and climbed over boulders, their dog, Rover, bounding along with them.

Cyrus was born on November 30, 1819, in Stockbridge, Massachusetts, and his parents named him after two men—Cyrus Williams, the local bank president, and Dr. Stephen West, the pastor of the Stockbridge church before Cyrus's father.

Six siblings welcomed him—David, Emilia, Timothy, Matthew, Jonathan, and Stephen. Cyrus was such a fragile baby, the neighbors thought he wouldn't survive. When he was learning to walk, he had to be placed in a bulky frame with wheels to support his body. Thin and wiry, the fiery little redhead ran on nervous energy.

The United States was recovering from the effects of the War of 1812 against Great Britain, and a few folks in town could still remember the Revolutionary War. Both of Cyrus's grandfathers were officers in George Washington's army. The year Cyrus was born, nearly ten million

Before the wooden ramp was placed here, Cyrus and his brothers climbed among boulders and down into this deep ravine, called Ice Glen, near their home in Stockbridge, Massachusetts.

people lived in the country's twenty-two states, and the population was growing. Cyrus's family grew, too. A sixth brother, Henry, and a second sister, Mary Elizabeth, were born in the next few years.

The Erie Canal opened when Cyrus was almost six years old. Traffic sailed up and down the Hudson River, and barges cut through to the Great Lakes. But Stockbridge was isolated, a small village near the western edge of Massachusetts. The nearest cities were miles away, and railroads didn't come through small villages. People drove oxen and horses over the rough dirt roads through the wilderness. The only inn in town was merely a stage-coach stop. With his brothers, Cyrus watched travelers change their horses and head farther west, to the expanding country.

Cyrus's father, the Reverend David Dudley Field, was a stone-faced preacher, strict but loving. His mother, Submit Dickinson Field, wasn't

The Reverend David Dudley Field, Cyrus's strict father, encouraged education for all his sons and daughters, but he had faith in Cyrus, despite Cyrus's lack of interest in school.

physically strong, but she dedicated herself to care for her nine children.

David, Cyrus's oldest brother, left to attend Williams College before Cyrus started school. A few years later, his next-oldest brother, Timothy, joined the U.S. Navy as a midshipman but suffered a lung condition and was forced to resign. He then embarked on a round-the-world voyage aboard a merchant ship, laden with cargo for far-off ports. Cyrus's older sister, Emilia, married a missionary and sailed to Turkey, where they served for two years.

Cyrus and Henry were buddies, being the youngest boys in the family. "At first we slept under the eaves, where we often heard the rain patter on the roof," Henry wrote. After Matthew and Jonathan left home, the two young boys moved into their older brothers' tiny bedroom. Cyrus slept on the bed, and every night Henry pulled the trundle bed out from beneath it and slept beside him.

Growing up in a religious home meant plenty of restrictions. Every morning and evening, the family gathered in the parlor, and each member in turn read a Bible verse. Then they knelt and Father stood over them delivering long prayers. Cyrus could hardly stay still.

On Saturdays, the boys raced home at sunset from wherever they were. Father claimed the Sabbath began at sunset, and they had better be home, or else. In his stern preacher voice, Father announced, "We are

Cyrus's mother, Submit Dickinson Field, raised seven sons and two daughters, working sometimes to the point of illness.

on the borders of holy time," and all work and play stopped for twenty-four hours. Mother even had to put down her knitting. Cyrus squirmed, waiting for Sunday's sunset, when he could play again.

Henry wrote, "How many, many times did my brother and I go out in front of our door, to watch for the sun's going down!" The minute it set, the boys bolted out to play.

Each Sunday, villagers filled the meetinghouse for divine services. Mother wore a white bonnet with a bow tied under her chin. The pulpit was so high that Father seemed extra tall when he stood in it. For a fidgety boy like Cyrus, the pews were too hard to sit on for more than two minutes, and services were long! On Sundays, there were three, and in good weather, parishioners picnicked on the village green between services.

Mother worked to exhaustion. She wove cloth from their sheep's wool, dyed it with vegetable dyes, and sewed clothes for her family. Most of the time, Cyrus wore hand-me-downs that his brothers had outgrown. Mother stood for hours at their open fireplace stirring the soup pot, and she baked tasty breads in their brick oven. They ate plenty of cabbage and potatoes, given as part of Father's meager salary. The children harvested other vegetables the family grew, and Mother preserved them. The Fields also received a generous supply of firewood, which Cyrus helped stack.

The boys shared a long list of outside chores. In summer, they weeded the garden, tended the sheep, fed the chickens, and took care of the family's horses. They took turns milking the cow. In the winter, they cut ice. And chickens had to be killed for food and packed in snow in the cellar. Cyrus cringed at that chore. He hated killing anything.

Life in the Field family was not all work. Cyrus loved their outings in the Berkshire hills. Mother packed picnics—baskets full of cheese, boiled eggs, dried beef, jam, and pickles. Cyrus climbed rocky peaks, scurrying to keep pace with his brothers. One mountain had a sheer cliff. Plus a waterfall. In winter, they enjoyed sleigh rides around the Housatonic Valley. Cyrus always had fun on summer visits to Mother's family in Connecticut. He and Mary Bryan Stone, one of his cousin's neighbors, spent hours together gathering seashells and pebbles and running along the shore, Mary's pigtails swinging.

Most of all, Cyrus liked organizing things and taking charge. He made up games and contests and convinced the neighbor children to compete—swim meets on the river, footraces on the village green, skating competitions in the winter. But he insisted on exact rules, and his need to win sometimes irritated others. Once, when a boy outran him in a race, Cyrus demanded that they run the race again, so he could be the winner.

He kept detailed lists: how many eggs each hen laid, how long each chore took him to complete, dates when different plants bloomed—everything. He became so good at keeping lists that, before he was twelve years old, Father assigned him the task of recording the family expenses.

The winter Cyrus was ten years old, he performed a special task. Mother became extremely ill and her raspy breathing frightened him. He slept in her room for weeks, listening fearfully for each breath. He kept a fire burning to keep her warm and gave her medicine every few hours.

The mild smell of wood smoke was comforting, but one day, walking home from school, Cyrus and Henry smelled a big fire. They dashed toward their house and discovered it was burning! Cyrus screamed when he saw neighbors throwing things out the window onto the lawn and run-

After the parsonage burned, Cyrus's family stayed with neighbors until this new one was built.

ning outside when the fire became too intense. Fortunately, no one was hurt, but after the fire, the family stayed with neighbors for months while another parsonage was built, this time out of brick.

Everyone in Stockbridge knew what went on in the pastor's family. And sometimes Cyrus's rambunctious behavior embarrassed his parents. Once, when Father couldn't find a missing rattrap, he told his sons to hunt for it and bring it to him right away. Cyrus found it while Father was preaching at an evening service. Clutching the trap, Cyrus burst into the meetinghouse, raced up the aisle, and plopped it at the foot of the pulpit. "Father, here is your rat-trap!" he shouted.

Neighbors expected Cyrus to succeed in school like his brothers had, but Cyrus didn't like school. He trudged to the two-room elementary school in Stockbridge, and later the academy upstairs, where he learned reading, spelling, geography, and arithmetic. He was good at arithmetic, but he was too restless to sit still through his lessons. And every day after school,

Cyrus endured more book learning at home. Father insisted on teaching all his children the Bible and Greek and Latin.

No matter what his nosy neighbors expected, Cyrus did not want to study law like David and Jonathan and Stephen, or become a minister like Father. He was not going to college. Just the thought of meeting the admission requirements overwhelmed him. His good character would pass, but knowing Greek grammar, parsing the work of Virgil, and writing in Latin—absolutely not. And he didn't want to be a sailor like Timothy. He thought the sea must be scary, with spooky creatures lurking below the surface.

Henry did so well in school that Father decided he could start college at age twelve. Their older brother Stephen had two more years of study at Williams, and the boys could room together. But now Cyrus's best friend would be leaving home. His younger sister, Mary Elizabeth, might go berrying with him, but he couldn't expect her to compete in swim races or go fishing or trap squirrels in the woods.

After Henry left, Cyrus became convinced it was time to step out on his own. He decided to go to New York City and find a job. David had settled there as a lawyer and would help him get started. First he had to persuade Father to let him go. He was not yet sixteen years old, but he was sure he could thrive. He ran to Father and presented his plan. Even though leaving home meant Cyrus would drop out of school, Father gave his blessing. "Cyrus, I feel sure you will succeed," he said.

Mother began sewing new clothes for him. Father handed him $8. They told him he would be welcome back home if he changed his mind, but Cyrus had made up his mind. Father then gave him two books from the family library: a Bible and a copy of Cyrus's favorite book, *The Pilgrim's Progress*.

On Tuesday, April 28, 1835, Cyrus wrote his last entry in the family's expense book. The next morning, Mother packed quince jelly sandwiches for his long coach ride west to the Hudson River, then an all-night boat trip to New York City.

"I HAD TO DEPEND
ENTIRELY ON MYSELF."

CYRUS WEST FIELD

3

THE BIG CITY

(1835–1838)

Cyrus bounced across western Massachusetts and into New York State in the horse-drawn coach, clutching his travel bag. April was nearly over, but leaves hadn't burst out yet, and the place felt barren. Every once in a while he took a bite of his quince sandwich to ease the pangs in his stomach. But they were mostly pangs of loneliness. Maybe he shouldn't have run off to seek his fortune far from home. Father assured him he would succeed in New York City, but now he worried.

When the coach reached the Hudson River, Cyrus transferred to a fifty-foot sloop and sailed toward New York City. All night, as home grew more distant, he squirmed in his seat. The ship was crowded with passengers and livestock, but Cyrus felt cold and alone. He yearned to reach New York, where David would welcome him. David was prospering as a lawyer in the big city. Their brother Jonathan worked in David's law office for a while, but he had left for Michigan to help form a constitution for its admission as a state.

Finally, daybreak. The minute the sloop tied up at the dock, Cyrus spotted David and jumped off. New York had already become the financial and business center of America, and it was growing—fast! Two hundred fifty

When fifteen-year-old Cyrus arrived in New York City in 1835, he found lots of activity around the docks. Merchant ships were loaded and unloaded, preparing to sail to ports all around the world.

thousand people crowded the city. Horsecars clip-clopped along narrow, cobblestone streets, but many roads and alleys were still made of dirt and were full of ruts, like at home. As Cyrus and David walked along the waterfront, they heard immigrants speaking different languages. Cyrus could see the tall masts of sailing ships coming into the harbor. David told him they brought elaborate silks and other exotic merchandise from Asia and Europe. Cyrus watched ships steam up the Hudson River, headed for Albany. Men there would transfer cargo onto barges to be pulled westward along the Erie Canal.

Cyrus stayed at David's house the first night. The next day, he walked to A. T. Stewart & Company, New York's largest dry-goods store, where David had found him a job as an errand boy. The store stood near City Hall on Broadway. The owner, Mr. Stewart, looked stern and was stiffly dressed, his beard neatly trimmed. Cyrus could barely stand still while Mr. Stewart spelled out his strict rules: No drinking, no theater, good manners, presentable dress. And he insisted on punctuality. If Cyrus showed up late to work, he would have to pay a 25¢ fine. "I always made it a point to be there before the partners came and never to leave before the partners left," he wrote. "My ambition was to make myself a thoroughly good merchant. I tried to learn in every department all I possibly could."

Cyrus would earn $50 the first year, and if that went well, his salary would be increased. *$50?* Cyrus added figures in his head. A rented room around the corner from the store cost $2 a week. That would add up to $104 a year. He could pay only half the rent! Right away, he had to borrow money from David. He hated owing anybody anything, but he desperately wanted to live on his own. He would work hard and pay David back in installments, with interest.

Cyrus's room in the boardinghouse didn't help his homesickness any. He unpacked his travel bag, hung up his Sunday clothes, and gazed around the room. Faded wallpaper made the place look drab, but the room had a small fireplace, so he wouldn't get too cold. He wasn't there much anyway. He worked six days a week, beginning before 7:00 a.m., often working late into the evening.

Sunday was Cyrus's favorite day of the week. He went to David's for dinner, which often included tasty foods like Yorkshire pudding or roast beef. Most of all, the lonely teenager treasured these family visits. Mother worried about him. She told another son, who was going to visit his brothers in New York, "Bring Cyrus home if he is still so homesick."

Cyrus received many letters—from Father, Mother, Jonathan, Henry, and Mary Elizabeth. His brother Timothy wrote that all was well. He was headed for South America, aboard a schooner, out of New Orleans.

When Cyrus wrote letters home, he always asked about Mother's and Father's health and sent greetings to Henry and Mary and his other siblings as they came home to visit. And he related news of his job. He kept detailed lists of his expenses and included them in his letters to Father: haircut, 12½¢; small bottle of turpentine to remove spots from his coat, 6¼¢; two papers of tobacco to put in his trunk to keep moths away, 12½¢;

Often homesick, Cyrus wrote many letters to his family in Stockbridge. In this letter to his mother, written December 14, 1836, he tells of brother Jonathan's appointment as clerk to a Michigan district court, and he inquires about family members, as he did in all his letters.

straw hat, $1. He explained that his old hat was so dirty, David thought he should buy a new one.

After living in New York for a few months, Cyrus wrote Father that Mr. Stewart expected his clerks to be well dressed, so he had his shoes mended for 18¾¢ and bought blacking for 12½¢. Clothes didn't cost him much, because Mother made suits and mailed them to him. Sometimes he bought fabric remnants and sent them to her for sewing suits. Once, when he needed a dress coat, he wrote to her: "I wish you would make for me, as soon as convenient, a black broadcloth *coat with skirts*, and covered buttons."

He did not write home about the hours he spent wandering along the shore, longing to sail upriver on one of the ships. Nor did he mention the times he attended the theater. Father claimed the theater was "an entrance to hell," and Mr. Stewart forbade it also.

Every now and then, Mr. Stewart held sales in the dry-goods store. He ordered the clerks to take merchandise off the shelves so he could mark prices lower to make the items sell quickly. When Cyrus wondered why he marked some below cost, Stewart told him, "The business is in keeping the stuff moving. Never have anything dead on your shelves."

Cyrus had lived in New York less than eight months when horror struck. On the night of December 16, 1835, a city patrolman in lower Manhattan smelled smoke and saw flames in the windows of a five-story warehouse. Quickly, he sounded an alarm. FIRE! Cyrus heard the City Hall bell clang. The tower watchman swung a lantern, pointing to the direction of the fire. Volunteer firemen raced to the scene in their horse-driven fire engines. Cyrus and thousands of others ran outside their homes to see what was burning.

A neighborhood near Wall Street was all ablaze. Cyrus watched flames spread quickly to hundreds of warehouses and stores, the places filled with expensive goods from all over the world.

As hard as firefighters fought, they could not control the raging inferno. It was -17 degrees Fahrenheit, so frigid that they had to drill holes through ice in the East River to draw water, only to have it freeze in the hoses on their hand-pumped fire engines. What little water the firemen could pump blew back onto them in the howling wind, drenching them and freezing their faces. Flames leaped from one building to the next, igniting whole streets. Barrels of turpentine standing on the East River docks exploded, and as the flaming fluid spread across the ice, it looked as if the river was on fire.

Cyrus kept staring at the blaze. The post office burned. The Merchants' Exchange, one of the finest buildings in the country, went up in flames. Eight men tried to rescue a marble statue of Alexander Hamilton in the rotunda, but the building started to collapse, and they barely made it out alive. The statue shattered when the building's cupola caved in on top of it.

The fire crackled with intense fury. Finally, at 2:00 a.m., U.S. Marines made their way across the icy East River with barrels of gunpowder from the Brooklyn Navy Yard. They blew up a few buildings that stood in the fire's path, and the pile of rubble kept the flames from spreading. Almost every building near the docks was gone. Some wharfs and ships were destroyed, too. Luckily, the fire didn't reach Cyrus's apartment, or other residential neighborhoods. Only two people were killed.

Cyrus wrote to his parents that the fire was "the largest that was ever known in this country." Flames rose so high, a yellow glow could be seen as far away as Philadelphia and New Haven, Connecticut. Near the heaps of rubble in the streets, the acrid smell of wet, burned wood lingered for days. And there was looting. "I was up all night to the fire," Cyrus wrote, "and last Sunday was on duty with David as a guard to prevent people from going to the ruins to steal property that was saved from the fire."

When it was over, 17 city blocks in lower Manhattan—more than 650 buildings—had been destroyed. Of New York City's 26 fire insurance companies, 23 were ruined. Reports said the fire probably started when a gas pipe burst near a coal stove. Damages amounted to more than $20 million.

Merchants began to build new warehouses right away. New York City was the leading shipping center in America, and with access to inner sections of the country through the Erie Canal, trade was booming. The merchants didn't want to lose that trade. And this time, they built their warehouses of brick and stone, not wood.

The country grew rapidly during the three years that Cyrus apprenticed in New York. The United States had more than 15 million people, with about 250,000 of them living in Manhattan. Michigan became the twenty-sixth state in 1837, adopting the constitution that Jonathan had helped write.

Cyrus wouldn't be a lawyer like three of his brothers, but he became interested in learning and often visited the Mercantile Library. Little gas-lights lit the reading room, where he read a variety of books, widening his

Cyrus had lived in New York City only a few months when a great fire broke out in lower Manhattan, destroying hundreds of buildings. Here, the Merchants' Exchange is blazing.

world beyond the Bible and *The Pilgrim's Progress*. Cyrus also enjoyed lectures and informal discussions at the Eclectic Fraternity. Every Saturday, he climbed to a fourth-floor room over a leather shop to debate issues and engage in lively conversations with the group. Even though he wasn't old enough to vote, he supported the Whig party.

At work, Mr. Stewart often walked silently through the store to check on his employees. Cyrus became popular with his fellow clerks when he started a *tap-tap-tap* signal to let them know Stewart was coming so they could appear busy. Cyrus showed such drive and energy, he was soon promoted to senior clerk, and he learned to handle difficult customers.

Stewart increased Cyrus's salary to $100 the second year, and he received another substantial increase in his third year. But he wasn't satisfied.

In 1837, while Cyrus was still working at the store, the country suffered a severe financial panic. Cyrus saw firsthand that all businesses could be vulnerable. Seven out of ten failed in New York City. Thousands of people lost their jobs and weren't able to pay their bills. A. T. Stewart & Company survived because it had not borrowed too much and had always paid its loans in a timely manner. Stewart's strong credit kept the company alive.

Cyrus worked hard at Stewart's, six long days a week, but he never overcame his homesickness. Every time he had any money to spare, he bought a ticket and headed up the Hudson River to go home. When his parents moved to Connecticut so his father could serve as pastor in his former church, Cyrus was disappointed. He had liked going home to Stockbridge.

At age eighteen, Cyrus moved back to western Massachusetts to work for his brother Matthew at a paper mill in Lee.

At least David lived nearby in New York City, and his brother Stephen had moved there to begin practice in David's law firm. Stephen and Father each received a degree from Williams College that year: Stephen in law, and Father in divinity (a doctorate). The only hole in the family was that no one had heard from Timothy—not a single word.

Cyrus was heartened that one brother lived near Stockbridge. With a partner, Matthew had bought a paper mill in Lee, Massachusetts, a few miles upriver. More and more paper mills were being built to meet the country's increasing demand for newspapers and magazines.

Matthew was a skilled civil engineer, but not an accountant. Cyrus was good with numbers, and Matthew offered him a job. Even though Matthew was eight years older, they always stayed close, and his offer was too tempting to turn down. Early in 1838, Cyrus told Father that he was moving to Lee to work for Matthew. He would earn $250 the first year "and my board and washing," he wrote. He planned to start working on April 1. But he needed to learn more about recording a company's financial records. A few months after his eighteenth birthday, he attended night school for six weeks to study penmanship and bookkeeping.

Cyrus resigned from A. T. Stewart & Company, despite an offer of a raise, packed his bags, and sailed back up the Hudson River.

"IN 1844 I WAS NOT WORTH A DOLLAR."

CYRUS WEST FIELD

RAGS TO RICHES

(1838–1853)

Cyrus opened the bookkeeping ledgers of Matthew's paper mill and went to work. Keeping detailed records came naturally to him, and he became a whiz at bookkeeping. A twelve-year-old boy occasionally showed up in the mill with his uncle, who operated another paper mill in town. Cyrus immediately liked the lad. Frederic Church, tall and thin like Cyrus, was also curious and adventuresome. Frederic lived in Hartford, Connecticut, and whenever he came to visit his uncle, Cyrus took him on hikes in the Berkshires. Frederic told Cyrus he dreamed of becoming an artist and wanted to paint scenery.

Hiking was a lot more fun than sitting still at a desk all day. Cyrus learned a lot about papermaking. But he was bored. He convinced Matthew to let him travel up and down the East Coast as a salesman—from Washington, D.C., to Boston. People liked Cyrus, and he persuaded many clients to buy Matthew's paper. When he could, he rode the new railroads. On one trip to Guilford, Connecticut, he became reacquainted with his childhood friend Mary Bryan Stone. She no longer wore her hair in pigtails. Mary had become a charming young woman. After that, Cyrus stopped in Connecticut every chance he had.

Cyrus married Mary Stone in December 1840. As the couple prospered, she and Cyrus entertained many people in their home.

Paper mills along the Housatonic and other rivers in New England were running full tilt. Cyrus wanted to advance in this fast-growing industry, and in the spring of 1840, he left Matthew's company and bought a part ownership in a paper mill in Westfield, Massachusetts. But not for long. "On October 1st of that year I was invited to become a partner in the firm of E. Root & Co., of No. 85 Maiden Lane, New York," he wrote. Root was a large wholesale paper dealer and appeared to be successful. Cyrus jumped at the opportunity.

On December 2, 1840, two days after his twenty-first birthday, Cyrus married Mary Stone at her home in Guilford, Connecticut. Father performed the ceremony, and Stephen was groomsman. The next day, Cyrus and Mary left by steamer for New York City.

Many businessmen were uneasy because of the financial panic three years earlier, but not Cyrus. His exciting new job was to promote sales on the East Coast—in Philadelphia, Baltimore, Boston, and other cities. The newlyweds rented rooms in a small house, which cost them $60 a month. They bought firewood from a street vendor and purchased whale oil for their lamps. North of the city, on the Croton River, a dam was being built, with a long aqueduct, to bring clean water to Manhattan. But it wasn't finished. So Mary drew water from a little pump at the corner of the street.

Just four months later, in April 1841, the company Cyrus had joined declared bankruptcy. Cyrus was stunned. "I was not the principal of the firm, yet on me fell the loss and the burden of paying its debts," he wrote. *How could he tell Mary he had failed and they were penniless?* Forcing himself to remain confident, he explained to her that they would pay what they could, and start over. They became extremely frugal, and, as always, Cyrus recorded their expenses. Some items on his lists were soap, 8¢; shoestrings, 5¢; the repair of a silk hat, 88¢; newspapers, 12¢; Dr. Paine, $1; pill, 6¢. His ledger for fall 1841 included $2 for a cradle. Mary Grace was born in October.

Cyrus labored for months to settle the affairs of the bankrupt company. Finally, he paid all his creditors 30¢ for each dollar he owed them. He hated not being able to pay everything he owed, but he covered his legal obligations. Then he dissolved the company and started his own paper-merchandising firm, Cyrus W. Field & Company, in partnership with his wife's brother, Joseph Stone. "I was not worth a dollar. What money I had made had all gone to pay the debts of the old firm," he wrote. Still, he trudged on.

Three of his brothers—David, Jonathan, and Stephen—were successful lawyers. Matthew had left papermaking to build suspension bridges in the expanding South and West. And his youngest brother, Henry, had

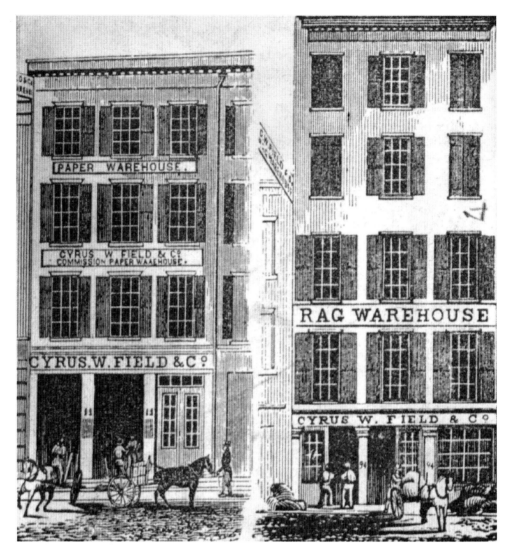

Cyrus W. Field & Company owned several warehouses, including some for rags to manufacture paper. To sell rags, Cyrus had to register with the city of New York as a junk dealer.

finished college and was now a minister. Cyrus wondered how he could succeed. He had learned a lot about paper merchandising and had made many business contacts. Knowing he would have to work long and hard, he resolved to be a successful paper merchant.

In 1842, the Croton Reservoir opened and the city celebrated. A new fountain in City Hall Park spouted water fifty feet into the air.

Cyrus became a fierce competitor. He was fair and honest, but he was sometimes sharp and dictatorial in business matters, always impatient to get things done. "All business intrusted to me was done promptly and quickly," he wrote. "I attended to every detail of the business, and made a point of answering every letter on the day it was received."

Recalling his days as a store clerk, Cyrus could not forget Mr. Stewart's advice to maintain strong credit and to keep merchandise moving. His office was located on Burling Slip, and the company's warehouses were close enough to watch carefully. They were near the docks where merchandise could be easily transported to steamers headed for the Erie Canal. Or goods could be loaded onto nearby railroad cars and sent by train to major cities. Two warehouses were for rags, a raw material needed for manufacturing paper. To sell rags, the City of New York required Cyrus to hold a license as a junk dealer.

In the mid-1850s, the Trinity Church spire, 281 feet high, is the highest point in New York City and dominates the skyline. Battery Park is seen at the tip of Manhattan, docks line the shores, and ships sail up and down the rivers.

Besides selling rags and other materials to paper manufacturers, his company sold paper to wholesalers—bond paper, colored paper, glossy paper, boxed stationery, and a new product, envelopes. Up to this time, letters were simply folded and sealed.

In 1842, the Fields found a house to rent farther uptown, on East Seventeenth Street, near Third Avenue. The Croton Aqueduct had opened, so Mary no longer had to haul water. Their second daughter, Alice, was born the next year, followed by Isabella in 1846. By 1848, the family included a fourth daughter, Fanny.

Cyrus worked so hard, his family rarely saw him except on Sundays. They attended church each week, and he liked to take them on afternoon excursions to Long Island or Coney Island or across the Hudson River to the woods in Hoboken, New Jersey.

The other six days, Cyrus jammed his schedule full, and he worked at a fierce pace. Up by 6:00 a.m. sharp, he was in his study by 7:00. There, he planned the day's work, read his mail, made lists, and followed them precisely. He wouldn't wait even ten minutes for the family to gather for breakfast. He said he'd lose ten minutes of work a day, which meant sixty minutes a week. That would add up to fifty-two hours, or more than two days a year, of wasted time.

As head of his company, Cyrus wouldn't delegate work if he could handle it himself. He seldom shared responsibility for business deals and contracts, even with Joseph Stone, his partner.

He also had strict rules regarding his mail. He refused to read any letter that came in the evening. If it brought bad news, he couldn't sleep, and if the news was good, he figured it could wait until morning. He destroyed any messages that he thought might cause pain to others or could be misunderstood.

New York City was growing rapidly. Five- and six-story buildings sprang up in lower Manhattan. Streets still reeked with plops of horse manure, but now the horses pulled railcars on tracks along Broadway. Telegraph lines began appearing.

Throughout the eastern United States, railroad construction was booming. Best of all, the paper industry was at an all-time high, and Cyrus W. Field & Company's sales increased steadily. Its three-year total sales from 1846 to 1848 reached more than $1 million, becoming one of America's major paper wholesalers.

Cyrus's incessant work took its toll. When anyone asked how he was, he replied, "Jolly," but he was worn out. He had never been physically strong, and before his thirtieth birthday, he looked thin and haggard, his face drawn. His doctor ordered rest. In April 1849, Cyrus placed Joseph Stone in charge of the company for a while. He and Mary left their four daughters with her sister in New Haven, Connecticut, and sailed to Europe to restore his health. Most of the eighteen days it took to cross the Atlantic Ocean, Cyrus was green with seasickness. But the moment they stepped onshore, he and Mary began an exhausting tour. For five months, they visited cities

Cyrus Field became a successful paper merchant and one of the wealthiest men in New York City.

in more than eight countries and enjoyed a cruise on the Rhine River before steaming home from Liverpool, England, in September. Industrial developments in England fascinated Cyrus. The country's trains, machinery, factories—all were more advanced than they were in the United States.

The year after Cyrus and Mary's trip to Europe, their fifth child, a son, Arthur, was born. That fall, Cyrus hired a buggy and covered wagon and took the family on a four-week vacation—a tour of Connecticut and his beloved Berkshires, returning by boat down the Hudson River.

About the same time, Cyrus bought a plot of land in a wealthy neighborhood on East Twenty-First Street and drew plans for a spacious four-story house. The Fields had lived in the Seventeenth Street house for almost ten years. He wanted a library for himself and something special for Mary. Because she loved nature and painted flowers in watercolor, Cyrus included a greenhouse for her—one of the first private greenhouses in New York City.

Their new home faced Gramercy Park. Cyrus's brother David built a home next door, and on the first floor, they cut a passageway between the houses. No one in New York City had ever hired a professional decorator, but Cyrus and Mary did, inspired by their recent trip to Europe. A French decorator furnished their home with Italian draperies, Persian rugs, and Greek statues. Cyrus's library had stone fireplaces at each end. His young friend Frederic Church had become an accomplished painter, and Cyrus chose two of his paintings to hang over the mantels. The house included rooms for the English butler and other servants. A stable was built out back for the family's horses and carriage and their cow. Each morning, the cow was taken to graze in a park near Madison Avenue. Like other New York City gentlemen, Cyrus now donned a black frock coat and wore starched shirts with high collars.

In 1853, while Cyrus worked at a frantic pace in his paper company, New York City was modernizing. Most streets were now lit by gaslight, and more of them were paved. Telegraph poles were a common sight, and wires spread along the East Coast and Gulf states. With a rapidly increasing population in its largest city, New York State passed a law to set aside more than 750 acres to create a park in the middle of Manhattan. The park was to be a green space for healthy recreational activities. A huge glass-walled pavilion was built uptown to house America's first world's fair, which opened in July. Exhibits came from everywhere, and tens of thousands of people flocked to see them that summer. The New York palace was modeled after the Crystal Palace in London, where the world's first exhibition of industry had been held two years earlier.

Cyrus's company profits continued to grow, and the firm had more than $300,000 in the bank. "There was no luck about my success," he wrote. "It was by constant labor and with the ambition to be a successful merchant." In 1853, when most New York City workers were earning between

Modeled after the Crystal Palace in London, this glass pavilion in New York City featured a high dome, fountains, and new innovations such as gaslights. In 1853, it held America's first world's fair, called the Exhibition of the Industry of All Nations.

$300 and $500 a year, Cyrus Field was worth more than $250,000. In less than ten years, he had made a fortune and, at age thirty-three, was one of the richest men in New York City.

Cyrus had worn himself out again, and his doctor prescribed rest. But something had gnawed at him for ten years. He remembered paying all his creditors 30 percent of what he owed as a partner of E. Root & Company, and he knew he was legally cleared of all that debt. But deep inside, he did not like owing anybody anything. That's when he looked up all the old claims and added the numbers. Early in March 1853, Cyrus mailed checks to every creditor for the remaining 70 percent he hadn't been able to pay earlier, plus 7 percent interest, totaling many thousands of dollars. Then he could retire.

A year earlier, Cyrus's younger sister, Mary Elizabeth, had married his business partner, Joseph Stone. It was time to turn the firm over to him.

At Joseph's request, Cyrus left his name as head of the company, added $100,000 to its funds, and left.

But Cyrus could not simply rest as his doctor ordered. He was intrigued by investment possibilities in South America and decided to explore mining in the Andes Mountains. And he had another reason to go.

"WHEN HE SOUGHT RELAXATION FROM EXHAUSTING BUSINESS CARES HE FOUND IT IN FATIGUING JOURNEYS, AND HE PREFERRED THAT THESE SHOULD BE AS DIFFICULT AND ADVENTUROUS AS POSSIBLE."

ISABELLA FIELD JUDSON,
DAUGHTER OF CYRUS FIELD

MOUNTAIN ADVENTURE

(1853)

Cyrus's doctor ordered rest, but to Cyrus, rest did not mean to sit back and relax. A new adventure was what he craved—even though it meant buying extra insurance because of his fragile health. He was searching for a new business venture, and when he learned that the Andes Mountains were rich with gold, silver, and emeralds, he couldn't resist. His friend Frederic Church would jump at the chance to go with him. Frederic could paint landscapes that would entice people to invest in a South American enterprise.

Cyrus had another reason to go there—to make one last attempt to find his brother Timothy. No one had heard from him for more than fifteen years since he embarked on a ship from New Orleans, headed for South America. The family had tracked down every clue, yearning to know what happened to him, still not able to give up hope. Cyrus had spent hundreds of dollars advertising in newspapers, offering rewards for news of his lost brother. The only promising lead came from a ship's captain, who told

Cyrus wrote detailed lists. This one, published in a biography written by his daughter Isabella, includes estimated expenses for his South America trip. Note that he planned to travel to Lima, Peru, and as far south as Santiago, Chile, and he had to pay an extra $100 premium on his life insurance.

the family he "had a shipmate named Field, whose father was a clergyman, and who had many brothers who were not sailors." That had to be Timothy. The captain claimed his shipmate was living in South America. Immediately, Cyrus and his brothers had written to officials in South American countries, but learned nothing. They had also sent letters to major cities, addressed to Timothy Field. All were returned.

Preparing for this trip, Cyrus secured letters of introduction from U.S. officials to take to diplomats and prominent citizens in Barranquilla,

Bogotá, and other cities, where he could inquire about his brother. And, as usual, he mapped out detailed plans, complete with a list of estimated expenses. His itinerary was filled with visits to gold, silver, and emerald mines, from New Granada south along the Andes Mountains to Chile.

Early in April 1853, Cyrus waved good-bye to Mary and the children, promising to be back in October, in plenty of time to take them to Stockbridge for the celebration of his parents' fiftieth wedding anniversary. They had moved back there after Cyrus's father retired. Cyrus and Frederic Church climbed aboard the ship *Viva* and sailed out of New York Harbor. Twenty seasick days later, they reached the port of Savanilla, New Granada, on South America's Caribbean coast. Barranquilla, their first destination, was fifteen miles away. No roads. Trekking along the narrow bridle path wouldn't be easy. The only horses Cyrus could find to rent were the scrawniest nags he had ever seen. For an hour and a half, they bumped along, sweating profusely and swatting millions of mosquitoes. Cyrus could barely breathe in the humid 100-degree-Fahrenheit temperature. In Barranquilla, thanks to one of the letters of introduction, he and Frederic were welcomed by the local diplomat and enjoyed a delicious dinner—roasted chicken, yams, mangoes, and rice. But no news of Timothy.

They had planned to take a steamboat from Barranquilla up the Magdalena River, but they missed it and were forced to wait ten days for the next trip. Frustrated by the delay, Cyrus wouldn't waste a minute. He scouted out the local marketplace, where vendors sold fish, meats, avocados, plantains, and lots of chocolate. Lizards darted along the ground, and he nearly tripped over turkey buzzards strutting around, pecking at garbage. "People in picturesque costumes were buying and selling," Frederic noted. "Donkeys were standing about with their immense loads and fish boats were arranged along the shore."

While waiting for the riverboat, the two men explored the area, hiking among giant cactuses, palm trees, and tropical vines. Cyrus gazed up, where he saw wasp nests as big as bushel baskets. Fragrant blossoms grew on trees and shrubs, and bright-green parrots screeched. Frederic

Cyrus and Frederic Church rode mules through miles of tropical jungle, with its buttressed trees and other exotic plants. At one point, Cyrus became so weak he could not keep going, and Frederic had to run for help.

delighted in making sketches of the sights, but Cyrus was anxious to move on.

Finally, on May 10, they boarded the steamboat, which bucked the fast-moving river current for hundreds of miles into the country's interior. Each night, they camped out in thatched huts along the shore. Bugs crept up and down the walls, and one night they spied an enormous tarantula, legs six inches long, crawling toward them. Frederic killed it before it reached Cyrus.

As the river narrowed, the current grew stronger, until the steamboat could no longer force its way upstream. A river guide poled them as far as he could in a canoe. They were still nowhere near any mines. Leaving the river, they rode scraggy mules over a mountain to reach one silver mine. Cyrus began to feel sick, but he wouldn't admit it to Frederic. Nothing was going to stop him from visiting the mine. "The superintendents showed us every thing of interest including all the process of separating the silver from the ore," Frederic wrote. Cyrus collected ore samples and asked Frederic to draw sketches of the machinery. There were plenty of mines in the Andes, and water power to run them from fast-flowing mountain streams, but Cyrus was discovering the sites were far removed from towns and hard to reach.

Heading for another mine, they rode the mules for days in hot, humid weather, zigzagging their way upward, through stands of scrubby trees and cocoa groves, into the mountains. "Soon after our departure it began to rain and night set in," Frederic wrote, "and on we floundered up and down through mud and water over rocks slipping right & left." After two and a half hours, soaked and shivering, they "arrived at a miserable hut." Exhausted, Cyrus refused to give up. He was determined to stop at an emerald mine at Muzo to see the brilliant green gemstones and collect more samples. After observing the mining process, they set out for Bogotá. Descending the mountain to the tropical jungle, the mules slipped over loose rocks, jostling Cyrus and Frederic in their saddles.

Jungle vines and branches were so tangled, the men lost their way. When Cyrus nearly collapsed, Frederic left him with the mules and stumbled about, hunting for the trail. Nauseated and dizzy, Cyrus felt feverish. Darkness fell, and eerie noises surrounded him. A hissing sound might have been a long, poisonous snake, and Cyrus was too weak to move. He cried out, but his voice was faint. Where was Frederic? What seemed like hours later, Frederic appeared, soaking wet. He had fallen into a stream, searching for a path. Cyrus couldn't keep going, and they bedded down right where they were. Frederic threw the saddles onto the ground for pillows, and they covered up with blankets. Not until they were scratching furiously did they realize they had camped on an anthill.

By morning, Cyrus was too ill even to sit up. Frederic ran for help. He could speak enough Spanish to recruit a few local people and managed to move Cyrus to Bogotá, another city where he had a letter of introduction to an American diplomat. They stayed in the diplomat's hacienda while Cyrus recovered, frustrated at wasting time. "Yesterday Mr. Field was sick," Frederic wrote in his diary on June 8. The next day he added, "Mr. Field is much sicker today but we don't know what the intermittent fever is." As soon as Cyrus felt a little better, he struggled into town. Bogotá was a bustling city, and he hoped to learn news of his brother, but he didn't. In the marketplace, he checked all the prices and inspected the merchandise—displays of sparkling jewelry, jaguar skins, clothing, and a colorful variety of fruits and vegetables. He couldn't resist purchasing some chocolates and a few souvenirs for his children. At the mines, he had collected ores and emerald samples, which he shipped home. As a special treat, their hosts took them to a bullfight, but it was much too cruel a sport for Cyrus.

Frederic knew of a spectacular waterfall named Tequendama Falls not far from town. On the Bogotá River, the water tumbled more than five hundred feet, much higher than the waterfall Cyrus had hiked to as a boy back in Stockbridge. Frederic wanted to sketch the falls so he could paint the scene in his studio when he returned home. Eventually, Cyrus felt strong enough to make the side trip. Frederic hired a number of men to cut the dense foliage. Chopping furiously with their axes and machetes, they cleared an area to allow a full view of the falls. The spray created a stunning rainbow, and Frederic drew a number of detailed pencil sketches.

But it was time to move on. They were already behind Cyrus's schedule, and he was edgy. With hundreds of miles still to go, he hired a local guide, Tomás, who insisted on bringing along his fourteen-year-old son, Marcos. For six grueling weeks, bony mules carried them up and down the Andes, Cyrus in search of mines, Frederic looking for scenes to sketch. They plodded through the jungle, then climbed to snowy mountain ridges. Their mules clip-clopped back down into the valley and up again into the high mountains. These were no Berkshire hills like Cyrus had climbed when he was young. Some spots along the rocky path came so close to the edge of cliffs, Cyrus feared the mules might slip and they would fall to their deaths. At times, they climbed so high, he could hardly breathe the thin air. "The guides were obliged to help Mr Field along," Frederic wrote. The high spots were also frigid, and Cyrus needed five or six blankets to stop shivering. Trudging back down into the steamy jungle, he stripped to one thin layer of clothing.

On their way to Quito, Ecuador, Cyrus and Frederic were arrested. Cyrus looked particularly suspicious because he was constantly peeking into places and examining items for sale. Authorities demanded to know what these foreigners were doing in South America and searched all their baggage. They thumbed through Frederic's sketch pads, which included drawings of Marcos as well as scenery. Not until Cyrus produced U.S. government papers were they released.

Frederic Church drew many sketches in South America, which he used to create exceptional paintings after he returned home. This sketch portrays Cotopaxi, one of Ecuador's highest volcanic mountains.

Wherever possible, Frederic stopped to draw sketches of volcanic mountains. While climbing above the tree line to view Puracé volcano, a pouring rain turned to hail, and they couldn't see anything. Soon after crossing the equator, Cyrus became ill again, but at least they could stay in a diplomat's comfortable estate in Quito. Still no word of Timothy. As weak as Cyrus was, after eleven days of bed rest, he insisted they move on. "Left Quito this morning," Frederic wrote in his diary. "Mr. Field is quite sick today."

They spent two days at nearby Cotopaxi, one of Ecuador's highest active volcanoes and a perfect cone. Frederic pulled out his sketch pad. Cyrus knew that his young friend was reveling in this Andean world, but the trip had taken much longer than they anticipated. It was September, and Cyrus grew more agitated each day. He had promised to be in Stockbridge on October 31 to celebrate his parents' anniversary. All his brothers and sisters would be there with their families, except Stephen, who was now living in California. Mary and the children would be waiting for him. There was no time to tour mines in Peru and Chile, as he had planned. He needed

Cyrus and Frederic had to cross the Isthmus of Panama in order to sail back to New York. The crossing included a trek along this mule trail.

to get downriver to Guayaquil, the nearest major port on the Pacific—fast! Irritated at the riverboat's delay, he and Frederic "hired a small canoe and paddled down to Guayaquil." Marcos came along. Cyrus was taking him to New York to educate him and return him to his homeland as a missionary.

After buying a few souvenirs in the marketplace, the three of them boarded the next steamship for Panama, where they would cross the isthmus and catch another ship to New York. No time for delays. But the railroad went only partway across the isthmus, and they trekked for miles on a rocky old mule trail. They reached Aspinwall on the Caribbean shore, only to learn they had to wait another six days for a ship. Cyrus became more frustrated when storms at sea delayed them even longer. Finally, late in the afternoon of October 29, Cyrus rushed down the gangplank clutching a leash with a young jaguar tugging on it, Marcos trotting alongside. Atop his baggage were cages of screeching parrots and parakeets.

They had been gone nearly seven months—exactly six months and twenty-three days, according to Cyrus's calculation. He had barely enough

Cyrus had promised to be home from South America in time to take his family to Stockbridge for his parents' fiftieth wedding anniversary. Four of his brothers and both sisters would be there with their families. This photo, taken later, shows six Field brothers: left to right, Cyrus, Henry, Matthew, David, Jonathan, and Stephen.

time to take his family to Stockbridge for the anniversary celebration. The most heartbreaking part of all was telling his aging mother that no one anywhere had news of Timothy or of the ship he sailed on. Not a trace.

South America was more of an adventure than Cyrus had expected. The mountains were rich with minerals, but there were no good roads, only narrow trails, making it extremely difficult to reach the mines. Transporting minerals through rugged mountain passes and thick jungles to the sea for export would be complicated and expensive. He decided investing in minerals was not worthwhile. But Cyrus refused to sit leisurely at home. He had no idea what it would be, but he would find something important to do.

"ONCE HE HAD GRASPED
THE IDEA, IT TOOK STRONG
HOLD OF HIS IMAGINATION."

HENRY M. FIELD

A TELEGRAPH
COMPANY

(1854)

Frederic Church sailed home from South America with plenty of painting possibilities, but Cyrus found no prospects for a new business venture. After returning from the family celebration in Stockbridge, he wasn't home a week before he became so restless he had to go to his office and check on his paper business. Joseph told him that company sales were continuing to bring in a substantial profit.

His paper company didn't need him, but Cyrus simply could not tolerate retirement. He was determined to find a challenging project. His brother Matthew had recently returned to New England after building bridges in Kentucky and Tennessee. He traveled to New York City for a visit. "I never saw Cyrus so uneasy," he wrote.

One day, in January 1854, Matthew met a rustic-appearing stranger at the Astor House, the luxury hotel on Broadway. The man introduced himself—Frederic Gisborne, an Englishman now living in Canada. An engineer like Matthew, Gisborne had strung telegraph lines in eastern Canada. He told Matthew about his trouble with a project in Newfoundland. A few years

Cyrus's brother Matthew met Frederic Gisborne here at New York City's prominent hotel, Astor House, in the winter of 1854.

earlier, he had formed a company and started building a telegraph line but had gone bankrupt and lost everything. Gisborne sounded desperate. To do any more work, he had to have money, and lots of it. Matthew immediately thought of Cyrus. He was convinced his younger brother needed something to do, and he had money to spare.

Matthew hurried to Cyrus's house and asked him if he would meet with a man to discuss financing a telegraph project in Newfoundland.

Cyrus knew telegraph lines were spreading over North America. They were becoming an important method of communication and provided a quick way to distribute news. At least seventy-five small telegraph companies had strung more than twenty-five thousand miles of electric wire in the United States alone. And more lines were being built all the time. But Newfoundland? That was a wilderness. Cyrus wasn't interested.

Matthew wouldn't give up. Would Cyrus at least talk with the gentleman?

Finally, Cyrus gave in to his brother's plea.

A day or two later, Frederic Gisborne followed Matthew up the wide steps to Cyrus's imposing townhouse. A servant answered the door and hung up their heavy winter coats. Cyrus welcomed the two men into his library. Mr. Gisborne began to explain his plan for a telegraph line that could speed up communication between Europe and North America. Standing beside the library table, Cyrus listened. In 1852, the Newfoundland government had granted Gisborne a charter, a legal document making his company the only telegraph company in Newfoundland for the next thirty years. Gisborne unrolled a map to show Cyrus the route. His plan was to build and operate a line all the way across the island—four hundred miles. It would reach from St. John's on the east coast to Cape Ray on the southwest corner, the closest point to the mainland.

Gisborne hoped that ships sailing from Europe would stop at St. John's and send messages by telegraph to Cape Ray. He planned to transfer them from there by underwater cable across Cabot Strait to Nova Scotia, then relay them to the United States by existing telegraph lines. Telegrams would reach New York at least two days faster than ships could arrive in port. And New Yorkers could save time sending messages to Europe. Gisborne told Cyrus that receiving information a few days earlier would be important to businessmen and government officials, both in Europe and in the United States.

Originally, Gisborne planned to use carrier pigeons or fast ships to cross Cabot Strait, which was the entrance to the Gulf of St. Lawrence. But two and a half years earlier, in 1851, two Englishmen had laid the world's first successful underwater telegraph cable. Twenty-five nautical miles long, it crossed the English Channel, connecting England and France. Gisborne now thought an underwater cable would be the best way to send messages across the strait.

Cyrus asked about the landline. Gisborne told him Newfoundland was such a rocky wilderness, they had hacked through only forty miles before his company ran out of money. Brutally cold weather and heavy fogs caused delays. Bears and wolves roamed the woods. The forest was so dense they could hardly pick their way along, much less cut a bridle path to lay a telegraph line. Several workers became ill, many had deserted, and one man had died.

When Gisborne failed to pay his workers, he was arrested, stripped of all he owned, and had an enormous debt of $50,000. His New York backers would no longer finance his venture. He needed money to pay off his debt, plus finish the job. Could Cyrus help?

Early telegraph lines and stations in the Newfoundland wilderness were primitive and unreliable.

Too restless to sit down, Cyrus stood, silently absorbing Gisborne's words. He knew little about the land to the north. But he politely agreed to consider the proposal and ended the meeting.

After Matthew and Gisborne left, Cyrus twirled his library globe until he found Newfoundland. He had never noticed that Newfoundland stuck way out into the North Atlantic Ocean. And Ireland stuck out on the European side. His eyes focused on the distance between them. "It was while thus studying the globe that the idea first occurred to him," his brother Henry wrote. *Why save only a few days in transporting messages? Why not lay a telegraph cable all the way from Newfoundland across to Ireland, and send messages instantly?*

First, Cyrus would finish stringing Gisborne's line across Newfoundland. Then he'd lay a cable to Nova Scotia to connect to telegraph lines leading to New York. That should be easy and wouldn't take long. With that accomplished, he could lay a cable across the ocean.

Cyrus was full of questions. *Would a long, underwater telegraph cable work?* No one had ever laid a cable anywhere near that long or in water that deep. *And what lay at the bottom of the ocean? Was it smooth or jagged?*

The next morning, Cyrus jumped out of bed and wrote two letters. The first, to Samuel F. B. Morse, whom he considered America's best expert in telegraphy. Morse had erected the first telegraph line in the United States, a forty-mile-long wire from Baltimore to Washington, D.C. Morse had also submerged a rubber-coated wire across New York Harbor. Cyrus addressed his second letter to Lieutenant Matthew Maury, head of the newly formed United States Naval Observatory in Washington. Maury had collected charts of the ocean bottom from soundings.

Samuel Morse quickly replied that an underwater cable was feasible. In fact, he had declared more than ten years earlier that an electromagnetic telegraph "may, with certainty, be established across the Atlantic." Clearly, Morse was confident that Cyrus's plan would work. Maury was optimistic, too. He had just completed a report which showed that the ocean bottom along the major sailing route from Europe to America was almost flat—perfect for a telegraph cable. This was great news!

All Cyrus needed now were a few other rich men to help him. Peter Cooper, his friend and neighbor, was one of the wealthiest men in the country. His companies manufactured iron and steel products, and he owned telegraph lines and railroads. An obvious choice. Cyrus's brother David warned him that Cooper probably wouldn't be interested. He was establishing Cooper Union, a free technical college, and was putting his time and money into that project. But Cyrus persisted. He knocked on Cooper's door.

It didn't take Cyrus long to persuade Cooper that a transatlantic cable would allow nations to quickly respond to each other, resolving conflicts peacefully. "Believing, as I did," Cooper said, "that it offered the possibility of a mighty power for the good of the world, I embarked in it." And they

In 1854, men gathered to form the New York, Newfoundland and London Telegraph Company. This reproduction of a painting by Daniel Huntington shows Cyrus standing at a table. Peter Cooper is seated at the far left, with Cyrus's brother David standing behind him. Continuing, left to right: Chandler White, Marshall Roberts, Samuel Morse, Huntington (the painter, who included his own face), Moses Taylor, and Wilson Hunt, a wealthy friend of Peter Cooper's who joined the group after Chandler White died.

agreed anyone who controlled communication lines would make a sizable profit.

Peter Cooper was highly respected, both for his business skills and for his generous donations to charitable causes. Having his support made it easy for Cyrus to recruit more people. Cooper recommended Moses Taylor, a wealthy banker. "I shall never forget how Mr. Taylor received me," Cyrus said. "He fixed on me his keen eye, as if he would look through me: and then, sitting down, he listened to me for nearly an hour without saying a word." Cyrus convinced Taylor to come on board. He recruited two other prosperous businessmen, Marshall Roberts of the shipping industry and

Chandler White, a paper merchant whom Cyrus had known for several years. David would be the lawyer.

The men met four times in March, at least once with Gisborne, offering to pay his $50,000 debt, and more if he would give up his company's charter. He agreed. Cyrus, Chandler White, and David set off for Newfoundland with Gisborne on March 14. They sailed to Halifax, Nova Scotia, then took a small steamship to St. John's, the capital of Newfoundland. For three miserable days, the steamer made its way north through blowing snow, hail, and a sea full of ice chunks. "It seemed as if all the storms of winter had been reserved for the first month of spring," David griped. Howling winds and rolling waves of course made Cyrus seasick.

At last they reached St. John's, where they were warmly received by the attorney general and the governor of the colony. They dissolved Gisborne's charter and created one for the new group. Gisborne's charter had not included any landing rights for underwater cables. Cyrus's brother David negotiated rights to telegraph lines across the island and landing rights for underwater cables from northern Labrador to as far south as Maine. The rights were granted for fifty years. This would block any competition.

Chandler White and David remained in Newfoundland to finalize the legal charter. Cyrus left to purchase a small steamship, which they would use to deliver supplies to finish the landline. As soon as they returned to New York, all the men met at David's house. On Monday, May 8, 1854, at 6:00 a.m., they signed the charter of the New York, Newfoundland and London Telegraph Company. Peter Cooper was elected president, and other officers were chosen. The group asked Cyrus to be the director to represent the company in England and Canada. Each man put in hundreds of thousands of dollars for the project, totaling $1.5 million. If successful, they would make huge profits. The entire meeting took fifteen minutes.

Once the new company was formed, Cyrus hired his brother Matthew to supervise the completion of the telegraph line across Newfoundland. Exuberant, Cyrus figured they could complete building the landline and lay a cable across Cabot Strait to Nova Scotia the next summer. They would tackle crossing the Atlantic the following year, in 1856.

But at the height of excitement, disaster struck. Less than two weeks after forming the telegraph company, Joseph Stone, Cyrus's brother-in-law, died unexpectedly. He was thirty-two years old. Joseph, Mary's younger brother, had been married to Cyrus's sister Mary Elizabeth for less than two years. Joseph's death also meant Cyrus lost his business partner, and he would have to take back the management of his paper company. He considered selling, but he wanted more funds for the cable project. More importantly, he needed a steady source of income to care for his family.

Just three months later, another tragedy fell on the family when Cyrus and Mary's only son, Arthur, died suddenly at age four. Despite Cyrus's sorrow, he plunged into the cable project.

The company directors met often around the big table in Cyrus's library. Most of the time, Cyrus stood, speaking quickly while pointing to his globe, his charts, and his maps. He pushed to complete the North American portion the following summer, 1855. "For months it was hardly possible to go there of an evening without finding the library occupied by the Company," Cyrus's brother Henry wrote. The family found it an "unwelcome intrusion."

Cyrus had to buy underwater cable for the Cabot Strait crossing, and it was manufactured only in England. It would be made of three strands of copper wire, twisted together, coated with insulation, and wrapped with iron wires for strength. Cabot Strait was sixty-five nautical miles wide, and Cyrus intended to order eighty-five miles of cable, to allow for extra.

He sailed for England in December 1854 to order the cable. There he met John Brett, who with his brother had laid the English Channel cable in 1851. Brett had since laid several more underwater cables. England was now linked to Ireland, Holland, and some islands in the Mediterranean Sea. Cyrus shared his dream plan with Brett, who had also thought about a transatlantic cable. Brett promptly bought a few shares of stock in Cyrus's new company, the first Englishman to be involved.

Cyrus also met Samuel Canning, an engineer who worked for Glass, Elliot & Company, a cable manufacturer. He recruited Canning to super-

All underwater cables were manufactured in England. Cyrus went to a factory like this to order cable to lay across Cabot Strait.

---

vise laying the Cabot Strait cable. His last task before returning to America was to contract for a ship to transport the cable to Newfoundland—a bark (a three-masted ship) named the *Sarah L. Bryant*.

"Who first conceived the idea of a telegraph across the Atlantic I know not. It may have been before I was born," Cyrus commented. But it was his dream now, and he was determined to make it happen.

"IT WAS A VERY
PRETTY PLAN ON PAPER."

CYRUS WEST FIELD

NEWFOUNDLAND

(1855–1856)

Cyrus's brother Matthew and his crew of six hundred men had been hacking their way across Newfoundland to string a telegraph line for nine months, since the company was formed in May of 1854. They worked through horrid weather and foul conditions. No wonder Gisborne had been unable to string more than forty miles of the landline. Clearing four hundred miles to build an eight-foot-wide trail to set up telegraph poles was a grueling task. Just surviving in the rugged wilderness was enough to discourage anyone. The men slept in tents or on the ground. They sloshed through torrential rains and fought hordes of mosquitoes all summer. When winter came, they were forced to climb over deep snowdrifts. Only in the stormiest weather did they stop working. The men built the trail close to shore in order to pick up supplies.

All supplies were delivered by the *Victoria*, the steamship Cyrus had bought for the company. Month after month, the *Victoria* steamed along the coast, delivering pickaxes, shovels, kegs of gunpowder, and barrels full of potatoes and pork. Crews dropped them off on rocky spots, where

The Newfoundland coastline is rugged. The telegraph company's steamship, *Victoria*, dropped off supplies on rocky points for the telegraph crew to pick up and take to their work sites.

the telegraph workers could find them and lug them to the trail they were building.

The minute Cyrus returned from England in March of 1855, he asked Matthew how many more months it would take to finish the landline across Newfoundland.

Matthew nearly exploded. "How many months? Let's say how many *years!*" He told Cyrus that in one half-mile stretch of road, they had to build bridges over three ravines. "You have no idea of the problem we face," he spat out. "We hope to finish the land line in '55, but I wouldn't bet on it before '56, if I were you."

Cyrus couldn't wait for Matthew to finish. Cable had already been purchased and would be shipped to Newfoundland in a few months, and Samuel Canning was coming from England to direct the cable laying this year.

The cable-laden *Sarah L. Bryant* was a sailing ship. Cyrus needed a steamship to tow it while laying cable, but he wanted more than a towing ship. For $750 a day, he chartered the smooth-lined coastal steamer *James Adger*. He invited family and about fifty prestigious friends to sail with him to Newfoundland to witness the first leg of his dream.

Crowds gathered at New York's Pier 4 on August 7. Horse-drawn carriages arrived, filled with bulky trunks and leather suitcases for the two-week excursion. Porters unloaded the baggage, and the ship's crew lifted it aboard. Men dressed in coattails stepped out and walked up the gangplank. Ladies in hoopskirts, some wearing bonnets tied under their chins, others with wide-brimmed hats or parasols, strutted along behind the men and onto the sleek ship. Two of Cyrus's daughters were the youngest guests, Mary Grace, almost fourteen years old, and Alice, two years younger. His other two daughters, Isabella and Fanny, nine and six, were not old enough to go. Cyrus's wife, Mary, stayed home with them, and she was nursing their month-old brother, Edward Morse Field. Cyrus's father, Reverend Field, and brother Henry and his wife boarded, as did his teenage nephew, Marshall Brewer, a son of his older sister, Emilia. Samuel Morse and his wife and son, Peter Cooper and his family, and Frederic Gisborne were among the other guests. John Mullaly, a reporter from the *New York Herald*, came along to write about the cable project.

The crowd waved as the *Adger*'s paddle wheels began to turn and the ship backed away from the pier. With a bright, shining sun, this promised to be the perfect excursion. *Adger* blew good-bye salutes and headed out to sea. "She was a swift ship," Cyrus's brother Henry noted, "and cut the water like an arrow."

Guests lounged on the deck of the *Adger* or in one of the spacious entertainment rooms. Cyrus had asked Samuel Morse to demonstrate the telegraph to the guests. When Morse brought out his sending and receiving equipment, they crowded around him. He tapped out "letters" on his sending apparatus, using the Morse code, a unique alphabet made of dots and dashes that he and his associates had created. The letters moved through the wire as sequences of short and long electric pulses.

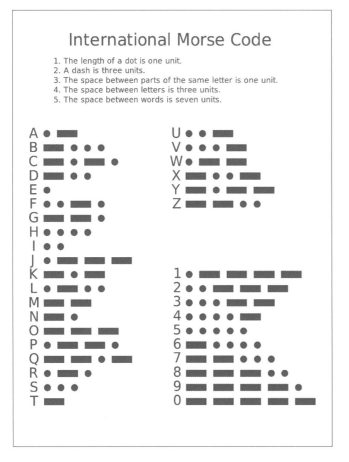

International Morse Code

1. The length of a dot is one unit.
2. A dash is three units.
3. The space between parts of the same letter is one unit.
4. The space between letters is three units.
5. The space between words is seven units.

Telegraph messages were sent through electric wires using this dot-and-dash alphabet code developed by Samuel Morse and his associates. Readers at the receiving end translated it. With a few changes, the code later became the International Morse Code.

Cyrus's guests were fascinated when they heard clicks at the receiving end, and Morse translated them into messages. The telegraph was not the only entertainment. In the evening, the guests enjoyed singing and guitar playing before they retired to their fancy private cabins.

The ship steamed along the coast of New England and Nova Scotia, headed for Port-aux-Basques, on the southwest corner of Newfoundland. There they would meet the *Sarah Bryant*, loaded with cable from England. But off the coast of Cape Sable Island, on the southern tip of Nova Scotia, they hit rough seas. As usual, Cyrus became seasick and rushed to his cabin. When the *Adger* finally arrived in Port-aux-Basques, Cyrus peered through his spyglass, looking for the *Sarah Bryant*. He could see forty or more wooden houses in the village, and in the distance Cape Ray, with a ridge several hundred feet high. But no ship.

Cyrus spotted Samuel Canning, who had just arrived from England. Canning told Cyrus he was worried. The *Bryant* had left England a month earlier and was long overdue. She must have hit bad weather. Canning knew that a five-hundred-ton bark overloaded with cable could easily go down in heavy seas.

Instead of idly waiting for the *Bryant* to arrive, Cyrus ordered the *Adger* to take him and his guests to St. John's on a goodwill visit to the colony's government officials. A few passengers stayed at Port-aux-Basques with Samuel Canning. Along the way, Cyrus gazed at the rugged Newfoundland shore with its jutting rocks, ravines, gulfs, and caves. Now he could see why Matthew's crew was still having so much trouble. Trying to build a telegraph line in this wilderness must be torturous. The *Adger* tucked into the port of St. John's through the Narrows, a channel bordered by high cliffs. A fortress guarded the entrance to the harbor.

In St. John's, Cyrus hosted a banquet on board ship for the Newfoundland officials. Later, the passengers went exploring, and many of them purchased huge black dogs and puppies. Native to the island, the Newfoundland breed was becoming popular among wealthy New Yorkers. The dogs were friendly, strong, intelligent, and great swimmers. "There were dogs on the quarter-deck, dogs forward, and dogs aft," reporter John Mullaly wrote. "Dogs in every coil of rope, and dogs basking in the heat of the smoke-stacks. Pups in boxes and baskets, pups in berths, puppies in ladies' arms and on ladies' laps. Go where you would, on board the steamer, dogs met you at every turn."

When they returned to Port-aux-Basques, Cyrus yelled to Canning from the boat: "Has the bark arrived?" A moment later, he saw the three-masted *Sarah Bryant*. At last they could start laying cable. But Cyrus soon learned the *Bryant* had suffered from a rough crossing. Repairs would take three or four days, and they needed to recoil the tangled cable.

Cyrus and Canning decided to change the spot for the telegraph station. Ten miles west, at Cape Ray, there was a more gentle slope and a sandy beach for landing the Newfoundland end of the cable. And it was a few miles closer to Cape Breton Island, the northernmost part of Nova Scotia, where they intended to bring the other end of the cable ashore. No roads led to Cape Ray to deliver lumber to build a telegraph house. Cyrus ordered the company's small steamer, *Victoria*, to load lumber and shingles and other building materials at Port-aux-Basques and deliver them. But the water at Cape Ray was too shallow for *Victoria* to get close to the beach. The crew built a raft and towed the lumber in by rowboat. They were still more than one hundred feet from shore when waves crashed against the raft and split it into pieces. Lumber was strewn everywhere, and men on the raft fell into the water. That's when the Newfoundland dogs on the *Adger* jumped overboard. They rescued the men, then clutched the boards in their jaws, one at a time, and swam all the cargo ashore.

By the time the crew finished building the telegraph house, a thick fog delayed them two more days. At last, the crew reeled the end of the cable from the *Bryant* onto one of the lifeboats. Men rowed as close to shore as they could, jumped into the surf, and pulled the cable onto the beach and up into the station. They pounded a log into the dirt floor and wrapped the cable around it to secure it.

Cyrus was itching to set forth. It was August 23. They had planned to be home by now, and they hadn't yet started to lay the cable. Canning wanted Cyrus to go with him on the *Sarah Bryant*. Cyrus left his daughters and his guests and joined him. The *Adger* connected two thick wire tow lines to the *Bryant*, each two hundred feet long. They had hardly started when one tow line snarled in the *Adger*'s paddle wheel, forcing them to cut it. A strong wind came up and blew the two ships about, terrifying the passengers.

The captain of the *Adger* corralled the women and children safely inside the cabin just seconds before the two ships collided. Cyrus couldn't believe what he was seeing. The captain "ran his steamer into the vessel, carried away her shrouds and quarter-rail," Peter Cooper said, "dragging the cable over the stern of the vessel." Cyrus grew more frustrated at the

A beach at Cape Ray provided the best spot for landing a telegraph cable.

further delay while men made repairs to the *Bryant*. Soon after repairs were completed, the *Bryant* veered dangerously close to shore, and Cyrus feared it would smash against the rocks. At the last minute, the *Adger* threw a line and pulled the boat away.

Finally, the ships started laying cable, and Cyrus's guests gathered by the rail of the *Adger* to watch. Moments later, the cable broke. Crewmen rowed the end of the remaining cable close to shore, hauled it to the telegraph house, and started over. It broke again. For the third time, the crew dragged the end into the telegraph house.

The next morning, August 28, all went well—for two miles. This time, the cable developed a kink, and they had to stop to untwist it. Cyrus began to wonder how they would ever make it sixty-five miles across the strait.

Samuel Canning had hoisted a flag on top of the telegraph house. He ordered the captain of the *Adger* to keep that flag in line with a mountain four to five miles behind it. That way, he'd be sure to keep a straight course and travel the shortest distance. The captain refused. He veered way off course, and the *Bryant* reeled out too much cable. By the time they were nine miles away from Cape Ray, the *Bryant* had already reeled out twenty-four miles of cable. They had eighty-five miles of cable on board, and Cyrus knew there wouldn't be enough to reach across the strait if the captain kept zigzagging.

Canning and Cyrus were on the *Bryant*, but Peter Cooper, the company's president, was aboard the *Adger*. He spoke to the captain about his erratic steering.

The captain's stiff reply to Cooper was, "I know how to steer my ship; I steer by my compass."

Cooper repeated his statement. "Your instructions were to steer by the flag and the rock on the mountain."

The captain would not follow orders. He "became as stubborn as a mule," Cooper said. Eventually, Cooper had a lawyer on board draw up a statement making the captain accountable if he still refused to obey.

To add to Cyrus's frustration, the cable became snarled. To make matters worse, the captain of the *Adger* sped up. He was supposed to keep his speed at 1.5 miles per hour, but he kept going faster and faster—much too fast for the crew to uncoil the cable safely. Canning raised a white flag to signal the *Adger* to slow down, but the captain didn't seem to care.

They hadn't laid half of the cable when a fierce storm whipped up. Waves crashed over the *Sarah Bryant*'s bow, soaking everyone on the deck. Men struggled to fix kinks in the cable, but nothing could fix the kinks in

A violent storm came up while laying cable across Cabot Strait. The *James Adger* (right) kept towing but nearly swamped the *Sarah Bryant* (left). The *Victoria* is shown about a half mile away.

Cyrus's stomach. Somehow, despite violent rolling and tossing, the *Adger* managed to keep towing, but it nearly dragged the *Bryant* under. Cyrus's frightened guests huddled inside the *Adger*'s cabins.

Another ship came by to assist, but in the howling wind, the crews couldn't hear each other yelling through their megaphones. The *Victoria* was within a half mile but couldn't help. The little ship almost swamped with its crew of forty men.

The ships could barely see each other, even when they were on the crests of the waves. They were two-thirds of the way across Cabot Strait when another kink appeared in the cable. The *Bryant* "rolled with such violence that the men could not work, and it was with the greatest difficulty they could even stand on the deck," Mullaly wrote.

Cyrus worried. He wanted his guests to witness a triumph, but instead they were in grave danger. Canning wanted to keep laying cable, but the captain of the *Bryant* finally convinced them that the lives of his crew were at stake. They had to cut the cable so the ship wouldn't be dragged under.

Cyrus watched it sink out of sight. The two ships headed for Sydney, Nova Scotia, where they unloaded the rest of the cable.

Bedraggled, the party arrived back in New York almost a month after leaving home. They took their dogs and left. The beginning leg of Cyrus's big dream was a total failure. The company had wasted more than $350,000, and all were discouraged. "We not only lost our cable by the unfortunate management of our captain, but came near losing the vessel, with all lives on board," Cooper said.

Cyrus Field was crushed but refused to give up. He declared they would lay the cable the following year. No towing. The cable must be laid by a steamship. And no impudent captain. Cyrus poured in more money and persuaded the other directors to do the same. He convinced Samuel Canning to try again, but Canning insisted that no passengers come along.

"Few had any faith in our scheme," Cyrus said. But he sailed to England again to order replacement cable. The next summer, in July 1856, the 80-horsepower propeller steamer *Propontis* laid the 1¾-inch-thick cable in 15 hours 17 minutes.

Matthew's land crew, with Frederic Gisborne's help, finally finished the landline from St. John's to Cape Ray early in October 1856. "It was a very pretty plan on paper," Cyrus said. "There was New-York, and there was St. John's, only about 1,200 miles apart. It was easy to draw a line from one point to the other—making no account of the forests and mountains, and swamps and rivers and gulfs, that lay in our way. Not one of us had ever seen the country, or had any idea of the obstacles to be overcome. We thought we could build the line in a few months." The project had taken two and a half years.

At long last, the United States was connected with the colony of Newfoundland by wire. A message could travel from New York to Maine, on to New Brunswick, to Nova Scotia, and across to the northern tip of Cape Breton. There, the telegraph line connected with the Cabot Strait cable to Cape Ray, Newfoundland, and four hundred miles of wire across to St. John's. This link was an essential part of Cyrus's dream to connect Europe and America. And they had just begun.

Cyrus and Peter Cooper and others had formed the American Telegraph Company, which bought dozens of small telegraph companies along the East Coast. This would provide a unified network to feed into the transatlantic cable as soon as it was laid and operating. Messages could go all the way from London to Florida. Cyrus and the other owners weren't the only ones consolidating companies. A new firm, Western Union, was swallowing up independent telegraph companies, expanding into the Midwest.

The cable project had already cost more than $1 million. Cyrus himself had invested a fortune. "Every dollar came out of our own pockets," he said. "Our only support outside was in the liberal charter and steady friendship of the Government of Newfoundland." John Brett, who laid the English Channel cable, had contributed, but Cyrus knew he now needed major support from Great Britain.

He was so weary that Mary became concerned. She knew he was determined, but if laying this short cable drained all his energy, how would he have stamina to lay a cable all the way across the Atlantic? But Cyrus ignored his fatigue and pushed on.

"I AM CONFIDENT THAT THE TIME WILL COME WHEN THIS PROJECT WILL BE REALIZED."

SAMUEL F. B. MORSE

CROSSING THE ATLANTIC

(1856–1857)

In July of 1856, right after the Cabot Strait cable was laid, Cyrus sailed to England. This time, he took Mary and his widowed sister, Mary Elizabeth, with him. They planned to tour while Cyrus held meetings. He met with John Brett and a telegraph engineer named Charles Bright, who had laid many miles of telegraph wire underground in England and a cable across the Irish Sea. The men decided to create a separate British company to raise money in Britain and to work together with the New York, Newfoundland and London Telegraph Company.

At least two large ships were required to carry enough cable to cross the ocean. Cyrus scheduled an appointment with Britain's foreign secretary, Lord Clarendon. Samuel Morse happened to be in London and accompanied him while he presented his plan. When Lord Clarendon asked him what he would do if the mission failed, Cyrus instantly replied, "Charge it to profit and loss, and go to work to lay another." Lord Clarendon smiled and asked him to write a proposal, which Cyrus did immediately.

While waiting for a response, Cyrus took Mary and his sister to Paris for a short vacation. He hoped it would lift his sister's spirits, but soon after they arrived, Mary Elizabeth died unexpectedly. Cyrus and Mary were shocked. It was the third death in their family within two years. Cyrus could not concentrate on his work. He and Mary spent a few quiet days in the English countryside, then he put Mary on a ship to New York so she could be with their children.

Together with John Brett, Charles Bright, and a fourth member, Dr. Edward Whitehouse, Cyrus officially organized the Atlantic Telegraph Company. Whitehouse was a surgeon who had experimented in electro-magnetism as it applied to telegraphy, and he became the chief electrician for the company. A few weeks later, they selected directors. One was William Thomson, a brilliant young physicist from Scotland. Scientists didn't fully understand electricity, but Thomson was known for developing theories to solve electrical problems.

In November, Cyrus received a letter from the secretary of the Lords Commissioners of Her Majesty's Treasury. Great news! Britain agreed to provide ships and pay for using the cable once it was operating—*if* the United States would do likewise.

The British government's approval gave Cyrus an extra selling point. He needed to raise money quickly in order to lay a cable the following summer, in 1857. Racing around Britain, he and John Brett introduced the plan to bankers and merchants. Cyrus promoted the cable by hosting elaborate parties for wealthy people and speaking to chambers of commerce in England's industrial cities.

The new company sold stock at £1,000 per share to raise £350,000. Cyrus wanted his countrymen to be part of the project, so he bought one-quarter of the shares to sell in the United States. The rest of the shares were offered for sale at the Liverpool exchange and other stock exchanges in Britain. People were so excited about the idea of a cable that all the shares sold in less than two weeks.

Cyrus was a terrific salesman, but he was no scientist. The company consulted a number of leading experts in England. One was Michael

Faraday, a famous English physicist and a pioneer in electricity and magnetism who had invented an electric motor and a generator. He had analyzed problems in early underwater cables. William Thomson had done so as well. The longest successful cable to date was not much more than 100 miles. A cable crossing the Atlantic would have to be 2,000 miles long. Dr. Whitehouse said a long cable would transmit strong signals if a high voltage was used. Samuel Morse, with Whitehouse and Bright, ran an experiment and proved signals could be sent through 2,000 miles of underground cable. They thought if it worked in the ground, it would work in the water. Their experiment satisfied Cyrus.

Some experts, however, doubted that a cable—submerged in water more than two miles deep—could function over such a long distance. Britain's Astronomer Royal declared it mathematically impossible. He believed that the pressure at such a depth would squeeze out all the electric fluid!

Confident that the cable would succeed, Cyrus pushed ahead. On the train, returning to London from a company meeting in Ireland, he met Isambard Brunel, a well-known inventor, railroad owner, and shipbuilder. Brunel seemed interested in Cyrus's cable project and offered suggestions. Later, on the bank of the Thames River, he showed Cyrus the enormous luxury liner he was building, almost seven hundred feet long. "Here's the ship to lay your cable, Mr. Field," he said jokingly. It wouldn't be launched in time for Cyrus anyway.

Cyrus was determined to lay the transatlantic cable the next summer. He and Peter Cooper and other U.S. investors had each spent hundreds of thousands of dollars on the project. The sooner the cable was operating, the sooner they would start getting their money back.

Thomson, Bright, and Whitehouse wanted to do more experiments to pick the best design for the cable. There were two problems: a long cable meant signals would be weak, and blurring of electric pulses had been noticed in earlier underwater cables. That made it difficult to tell the difference between a dot and a dash of the Morse code. People had a hard time reading messages. Thomson and Faraday believed the blurring hap-

Gutta percha insulation is applied to strands of copper wire.

pened because seawater conducted electricity. But Cyrus said there wasn't time to conduct more tests.

He headed for the Gutta Percha Company, a cable manufacturer in London. There, he watched copper wires being wound together, and he sniffed a foul-smelling raw material boiling in huge vats. The gum, called gutta percha, came from a tropical tree discovered near Singapore, which was under British rule. Scientists had learned that when they heated gutta percha, it softened and they could mold it into any shape they wanted. When it cooled, it kept that shape. Best of all, it made an excellent insulator for underwater cables.

Cyrus ordered 2,500 nautical miles of cable, which included enough for slack, to cover the irregular ocean bottom. He pushed for completion by the end of June, because summer was the best time to sail across the Atlantic Ocean. Then, worn out, he sailed home, hoping to spend a quiet Christmas with Mary, who was expecting another child, and their family.

Cyrus had just unpacked his bags when he learned that the Cabot Strait cable had broken. Not only that, the landline in Newfoundland was in a shambles. Without the Newfoundland connection, his dream plan was dead. He had intended to go to Washington, D.C., right after New Year's Day to seek U.S. support to match Britain's agreement. That would have to wait. He left for Newfoundland immediately. Quickly, he recruited a new superintendent to repair and manage the system. While in St. John's, he arranged for the legislature to grant the new British company the same privileges his brother David had arranged in 1854. But keeping such a relentless pace took its toll. Cyrus collapsed from fatigue and became so ill a doctor ordered him to bed. Refusing to stay, he caught the next ship for New York.

Before hardly taking a breath at home, he set off for Washington, D.C. The British navy had agreed to supply one ship to lay a cable, but only if the United States would supply the other. It was essential that he borrow a Navy ship, and the U.S. Congress had to approve the loan. Peter Cooper had already written a letter to President Franklin Pierce, making the request. When Cyrus arrived, he found that Cooper's letter had convinced the president and New York senator William Seward to support the plan. In January 1857, Seward wrote a bill and presented it to the Senate and the House of Representatives to grant the requests Cooper had made.

Despite the enthusiasm of a few, Cyrus faced tough opposition in both houses of Congress. The United States was not on friendly terms with Great Britain. In the previous eighty years, the two countries had fought the Revolutionary War and the War of 1812, both on U.S. soil, and some congressmen worried about another war. Many thought Britain should pay the entire bill. After all, both Ireland and Newfoundland were in British territory. Others argued that if Britain controlled a transatlantic cable entirely, the United States would be left out.

Senator Seward agreed with Cyrus's desire for peace. Seward spoke to the other senators. "My own hope is, that after the telegraphic wire is once laid, there will be no more war between the United States and Great Britain. I believe that whenever such a connection as this shall be made, we diminish the chances of war."

The USS *Niagara* left the Brooklyn Navy Yard for England in April 1857. Launched just two years earlier, the 328-foot-long wooden warship had an iron frame.

Senator Stephen Douglas of Illinois spoke in favor of loaning ships. "England tenders one of her national vessels," he said, "and why should we not tender one also?"

But most congressmen were opposed. Cyrus wore himself out speaking individually with almost every member of Congress, trying desperately to convince each one about the importance of the cable and the need for government support. Debate dragged on for weeks.

"Those few weeks in Washington were worse than being among the icebergs off the coast of Newfoundland," Cyrus's brother Henry wrote. The cable was never "entangled in such a hopeless twist as when it got among the politicians."

Finally, the bill passed the House of Representatives by nineteen votes. Two weeks later, Cyrus sighed in relief when the bill passed the Senate—

by a single vote. The United States would furnish two of its best Navy ships, the USS *Niagara* to lay half the cable and the USS *Susquehanna* as a support ship. Cyrus stood by President Pierce when he signed the bill on March 4, 1857, just hours before leaving office.

Cyrus tried to sell his shares in the British company to Americans, but he discovered that most people were skeptical of his plan. Many thought he and Cooper and the other promoters were crazy fools, wasting vast amounts of money on a ridiculous idea. They didn't believe it could work, and only a few were willing to invest in the project. Cyrus had to keep the remaining shares himself, which amounted to more than $300,000. That, plus the money he had already put into the project, was most of his assets. But the disgruntled opinions didn't stop him. Cyrus stayed home for a few days after Mary gave birth to Cyrus William in March to be sure she and the baby were healthy. Then he hurried back to England.

Cable production had already begun in February 1857. It was being made in two parts, the inner core and an outer protective layer.

This cable was better than the Cabot Strait cable. The conducting part of the inner core was a strand of seven copper wires instead of three. Six wires were twisted around a center wire. The wires were coated with the smelly gutta percha, then wrapped in hemp soaked in a mixture of tar, pitch, linseed oil, and beeswax. The design disturbed William Thomson. He wanted a purer grade of copper, but it was too late to change the cable specifications.

The cable was manufactured in sections and joined into one-hundred-mile lengths. As fast as they were made, Dr. Whitehouse tested them to see if they conducted current. The lengths were then wound onto reels for shipment to another factory to have the protective layer applied.

To be certain the cable would be ready to lay that summer, two factories applied the protective layer. Half of the reels were shipped to a factory near London, the other half near Liverpool. Both companies wrapped the insulated copper core with 18 strands of iron wire, each strand made of 7 wires, twisted together. They coated the whole thing with a thick tar mixture. Cyrus figured 7 wires times 18 strands meant 126 wires would be protecting the cable. He was frustrated when he learned that the two factories wound the wires in opposite directions. One spiraled to the right, the other to the left, which meant the cable would untwist when the ends were spliced together. Workers quickly designed a special device to make sure the splice would hold.

The cable was heavy. Every nautical mile of cable weighed a ton, and there were 2,500 miles of it. And an even heavier shore-end cable weighed more than nine tons per mile. The shore ends were stronger so they wouldn't become snagged by ships' anchors or fishermen's trawlers, or be shifted by powerful tides. A ten-mile length was required for the coast of Ireland, fifteen for Newfoundland.

The *Niagara* left New York for England on April 24, 1857. It was the largest steam frigate in the world and the finest ship in the U.S. Navy. Because this was a peaceful mission, the space where its big cannons would have been was cleared, and a few bulkheads, or walls, had been removed to make room for the cable. The only guns on deck were four small cannons to signal messages to other ships. The side-wheel steamer *Susquehanna* was pulled from duty in the Mediterranean Sea.

Britain provided three ships: the HMS *Agamemnon* to lay half the cable, HMS *Leopard* to assist, and HMS *Cyclops* to lead the fleet and take ocean soundings. Previous soundings had located a steep drop-off about two hundred miles off the coast of Ireland. Cyrus and the other company direc-

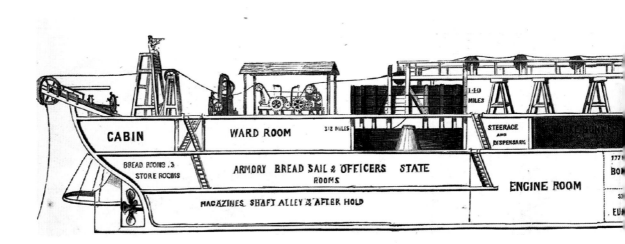

tors wanted more details. Sudden depth changes would affect how the cable should be reeled out, and Cyrus didn't want anything to go wrong. Earlier sounding crews had collected samples of soil from the ocean floor. They scooped up soft ooze, made of microscopic shells, and Cyrus was assured it would make an ideal bed for a cable.

Shipyard workers made room for giant tanks to hold the cable on both the *Niagara* and the *Agamemnon*. More open space was needed on the *Niagara*, and sections of the crew's quarters were removed. A huge area in *Agamemnon*'s midships would hold most of her half of the cable. To keep the cable from getting caught, a propeller cage was attached at the stern of each ship. And both ships were outfitted with bulky paying-out machinery to lay the cable, including a brake to control the speed. Cyrus saw where the cable would wind around four wheels, each one with grooves to keep the cable from slipping. The cable would run out to a fifth wheel just over the stern of the ship, before dropping into the ocean.

Niagara's half of the cable was loaded in Liverpool, the *Agamemnon*'s in London. It took 120 volunteers three weeks to load it onto the ships. They took turns, 30 men at a time, coiling the cable into the circular tanks. One man walked round and round in the tank, handing the cable to coilers stationed at the edges, piling layer upon layer. By the third week of July, the cable was loaded. The ships sailed for Ireland.

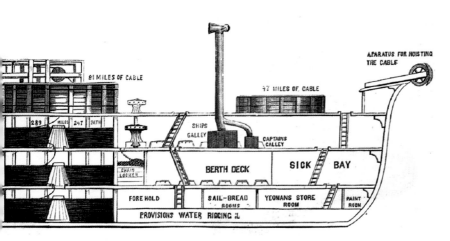

Seven large tanks were built on several decks of the *Niagara* to hold the cable. The four tanks on the lower decks are shown with white cones in the center. A cage was built at the stern to keep the cable from becoming caught in the propeller.

The propeller-driven, three-masted British warship HMS *Agamemnon* carried one-half of the cable.

Dr. Whitehouse said he wasn't well enough to sail on the cable-laying expedition but would stay at the telegraph station in Ireland. William Thomson could take his place. Cyrus was in good hands. Joining him on the *Niagara* were Charles Bright, chief engineer; William Everett of the U.S. Navy, engineer of the *Niagara* and assistant to Bright; and Samuel Canning. John Mullaly, the *New York Herald* correspondent who had sailed across Cabot Strait with Cyrus, was on board also. Samuel Morse joined the group, but he became sick and couldn't help.

The fleet met at Queenstown, on the south coast of Ireland, on July 30. The *Niagara* and *Agamemnon* were moored three-quarters of a mile apart, and their cables were spliced together temporarily so Whitehouse could test the entire length. The electric current ran perfectly! Early the next morning, Cyrus sent a message to the Associated Press in Liverpool: "The Submarine Cable on board the Niagara and Agamemnon, over twenty-five

This drawing shows the cable machinery used on both the *Niagara* and *Agamemnon*. The cable wound around the wheels, passed through the dynamometer and brake, and out over a stern wheel, where it dropped into the ocean. Here, the brakeman turns a wheel to adjust the brake and control tension.

hundred miles long, was joined together last evening, and messages were sent through its entire length in less than a second. Everything works beautifully, and we are all in high spirits."

At the last minute, Dr. Whitehouse decided to change the plans, causing a frustrating delay. Cyrus and Bright intended for the two cable ships to meet in mid-ocean, splice their cables together, then start reeling them out. They would steam in opposite directions, *Agamemnon* toward Ireland, *Niagara* toward Newfoundland. Once the cable was connected, the ships would be able to keep in contact with each other, but not with Ireland. Whitehouse, who was staying at the telegraph station, insisted on keeping in constant contact with the ship that was laying the cable. After much opposition, Cyrus and Bright gave in to Whitehouse. *Niagara*'s half would be laid first. In mid-ocean, the crews would splice the end of *Niagara*'s cable to *Agamemnon*'s half and *Agamemnon* would lay the rest of it. Whitehouse could receive progress reports all the way across the ocean.

Crews in small boats grab the tip of the shore-end cable from the *Niagara*, ready to row it to steamships, which will lay it into a cove at Valentia.

The ships then sailed to Valentia Island on Ireland's west coast. Charles Bright had earlier surveyed that shoreline for a landing site. He chose Valentia because it was sheltered from heavy seas. On August 5, two small steamships brought the heavy shore-end cable into a little cove. Smaller boats then towed one end closer to shore. In the shallow water, sailors carried it through the surf and pulled it to a temporary cable house. Hundreds of excited well-wishers grabbed hold and pulled with them, tar smearing all over their hands.

The next day, the fleet finally set sail for Newfoundland. Cyrus spoke to the crowd: "Ladies and gentlemen, Words cannot express to you the feelings within this heart." He extended an American welcome to the crowd, many of whom had relatives who had emigrated to the United States during the potato famine a few years earlier. He ended his short speech with, "What God has joined together, let no man put asunder." The crowd roared with cheers. His Excellency, the Lord Lieutenant of Ireland, Earl of

Carlisle, extended good wishes, and the vicar of the parish offered prayer. Two thousand people waved good-bye.

The *Niagara*'s crew was split into two watches, each four hours long. Men were stationed on deck to make sure the cable stayed in line. Still, after five miles, the shore-end line caught in the machinery and broke. The *Niagara* had to go back. Cyrus paced the deck while ships retrieved the cable. They spliced it and started again, very slowly, to avoid another accident.

Eight miles out, they spliced the shore end to the main cable. The *Niagara* now sped up to five knots, and the electricians began sending messages back to shore. They sent electrical signals to the telegraph station at Valentia at scheduled times to make sure the line was working. Cyrus and the officers could also send messages.

Lifeboats and life buoys were lined up along the deck. Men stationed on the poop deck at the stern kept careful watch. If anyone fell overboard, they would release a life buoy at once. Sometimes Cyrus stood there and watched the cable drop steadily into the sea.

Crew's quarters were crowded, now that the *Niagara* had been refitted to make room for tons of telegraph cable. Cyrus, the engineers, electricians, and the ship's officers bunked in tiny bedrooms. Sailors slung hammocks to sleep in when they were off watch. The officers ate in a mess hall, but the sailors ate on a lower deck, in groups of fifteen. They spread canvas tarps on the floor for tablecloths and sat cross-legged around them. A few fiddlers among the crew scratched out tunes. The minute the cook set a big pot of dinner down in the center of the tarp, the hungry sailors grabbed their spoons and scooped food onto their plates, scarfing down whatever was served, mostly stew and bread, pork, beef, and potatoes. One concoction, called "dunderfunk," was meat and beans, mixed with hard bread, molasses, and a little vinegar.

Up on the top deck, the paying-out machinery grumbled like a coffee grinder, making a constant racket. Yet its rhythm was a strange comfort. Whenever the "old coffee-mill" stopped, everyone ran on deck to see what went wrong. Tar could harden in the grooves, which sometimes threw

Men on the *Niagara* reel out cable from a tank on the top deck, careful to keep it from kinking. *Agamemnon* and support ships are visible in the background.

the cable off the wheels. The ship would have to be stopped, the cable clamped, and the tar softened with oil. Or the cable could kink and have to be straightened. Or it could snap with no warning. No matter what caused the machinery to stop, Cyrus and everyone else became alarmed. The fear of losing the cable "haunted us like a nightmare," reporter Mullaly wrote. "Not a word was spoken except by those in command."

On Sunday, the captain held a divine service for all who were not on duty. At noon on Monday, the fifth day out, they were 214 miles from shore, and had reeled out 255 miles of cable. Bright wrote: "At 4 o'clock in the morning of the 10th the depth of water began to increase rapidly from 550 fathoms to 1,750 in a distance of eight miles." That's when things became tricky. The brakeman had to carefully watch how fast the cable was reeling out. As the ocean deepened, the weight of more cable hanging off the ship made it pull harder and the crew didn't want it to get out of control. But applying the brakes too quickly or too strongly would snap the cable. Fortunately, the brakes worked well.

The water kept getting deeper. "At this time we were in 2,150 fathoms water, and the cable was going out in magnificent style," Mullaly wrote. Cyrus knew a fathom was six feet. That meant the water was now almost 2½ miles deep. And the electric current was still flowing!

Dr. Whitehouse, at the Valentia station, forwarded a message from the ship to newspapers: "All well on board. Moderate westerly wind. All more and more trustful of complete success."

Suddenly, at 9:00 p.m., the electrical current stopped. The electricians worked frantically for more than two hours to fix it. But they couldn't. They had just decided to cut the cable and reel back in what had been laid when the signal mysteriously returned. "You could see the tears standing in the eyes of some as they almost cried for joy," Mullaly wrote.

But no one could explain why it happened, and unexplainable problems made Cyrus nervous. The ship became strangely silent. Cyrus went to bed, exhausted, but he couldn't sleep. Shortly before daybreak, he heard commotion on deck.

Charles Bright came to Cyrus's door, trembling. "The cable's gone," he said.

Cyrus stood up, numb.

The cable sank more than two miles to the bottom of the sea.

Bright told Cyrus he had stepped away from the machine for only a few minutes. He left a mechanic in charge, who either didn't adjust the brake wheel at all or turned it the wrong way when the ship rolled on a wave. The strain on the cable made it snap.

Cyrus ran on deck and gazed out over the water. The broken end of the cable hung over the stern wheel, swinging loosely. One-half a million dollars' worth of cable was lost in a fraction of a second. And Cyrus's dream was sinking.

In less than five minutes, the entire crew was on deck, stunned. The machinery had stopped grinding, and an eerie silence hovered over the ship. Men stared at each other in disbelief.

Cyrus remained calm. He wasn't going to quit now. Having suffered defeat plenty of times, he was all the more determined to succeed. *Surely a cable would work!* They had laid nearly four hundred miles of cable before it broke. And electric current had flowed well when the cable was in deep water. "Losing no time in vain regrets, he called a meeting at once on board the Niagara," Mullaly wrote.

The captain signaled the other ships in the fleet, and their captains came aboard. Cyrus told them he refused to give up. As soon as possible, he intended to try again. He asked the two cable ships to stay in mid-ocean for a few days to try splicing *Niagara*'s remaining cable with the cable on the *Agamemnon* and check for current. And he requested more ocean soundings.

The ships lowered their flags to half-mast. Cyrus boarded the HMS *Leopard* and headed for London to call a meeting of the directors of the Atlantic Telegraph Company. On board the *Leopard*, Cyrus wrote a letter to his family to tell them the sad news. But he assured them, "My confidence was never so strong as at the present time, and I feel sure, that with God's blessing, we shall connect Europe and America with the electric cord." He added, "Do not think that I feel discouraged, or am in low spirits, for I am not."

Newfoundland eagerly awaited the fleet's arrival. A new telegraph station was ready in Bull's Arm, at the head of Trinity Bay. St. John's planned a celebration. The company's paddle steamer, *Victoria*, was ready to welcome the fleet. Everyone waited. Day after day, people scanned the horizon, searching for the *Niagara*. St. John's finally sent out a news item, which appeared in New York's *Evening Post* on August 25: "There are no signs at Trinity Bay of the Atlantic telegraph fleet." Eventually, newspapers reported that the cable had broken and the fleet had returned to England.

Two days later, the *New York Herald* published a message from Cyrus. "Although the unfortunate accident will postpone the completion of this great undertaking for a short time," he reported, "there appears to be no great difficulty in laying down the cable; and it has been clearly proved that you can telegraph successfully through twenty-five hundred miles of cable."

The company directors decided they couldn't make a second attempt that year. Almost four hundred miles of cable had been lost. There was not enough to finish the work and there wasn't time to manufacture more and lay it before autumn storms swept across the North Atlantic. They also needed to redesign the paying-out machinery and put safety mechanisms in place. And the crew must be better trained.

The two cable ships returned to Plymouth, England, unloaded the cable into tanks on shore, and returned to duty in their respective navies. A few months later, Bright recovered fifty miles of cable in a small paddle steamer to reuse the next year.

Cyrus focused on next year's plans. The company had lost cable, time, and an enormous amount of money. And the public on both sides of the Atlantic no longer had faith in the project. A writer for the Brooklyn *Eagle* wrote, "We cannot see how any hope of the success of the enterprise can be entertained. On the contrary, we must look upon it as one of those things which cannot be done."

When Cyrus arrived home in December 1857, he was surprised to find his paper company nearly bankrupt. The United States was in another financial panic. If Cyrus hadn't been spending so much time and energy on the cable project, he might have seen clues. In the past few years, jobs had been plentiful, and buying and selling had increased, particularly in the West, where population was growing rapidly. Railroads and real estate boomed. But when expansion slowed down, companies couldn't make loan payments to banks, and the banks struggled with insufficient money to operate. To make matters worse, in September, a steamship sank off Cape Hatteras, North Carolina, in a hurricane. It was filled with a huge shipment of gold from California. New York banks were depending on that delivery and, as a result, many failed. This slowed the entire economy and the stock market crashed. Cyrus W. Field & Company couldn't pay its bills because companies who owed it money couldn't pay. Cyrus took some goods off his shelves and returned them to suppliers. He wrote legal notes to his other suppliers, promising payment with interest as soon as possible.

Cyrus needed his paper company to be healthy to support his family, and he was in a hurry to gather financial support for the next cable expedition. He feared economic recovery would be slow, making both goals difficult. Cyrus held on to his dream, but he wondered how he could make it happen.

"WHILE ALL HOPED
FOR SUCCESS, NO ONE
DARED TO EXPECT IT."

HENRY M. FIELD

TRY AGAIN

(1858)

Cyrus Field had not a moment to lose. It didn't matter that his own fortune had collapsed. Or that he couldn't find additional investors for the cable after the 1857 failure. Cyrus felt pressure from competitors. One in particular, Taliaferro Shaffner, owner of several telegraph lines in the Midwest, showed interest in oceanic cables and tried to persuade Newfoundland to cancel Cyrus's fifty-year exclusive landing rights.

Cyrus pushed on. In December 1857, he traveled to Washington, D.C., again and managed to secure the same two Navy ships for another attempt. He also arranged a leave of absence for U.S. Navy engineer William Everett to redesign the cable-laying machinery. A month later, he sailed back to England with Everett.

In early fall 1857, the British company directors had begun preparations for their next attempt and held frequent conferences. Cyrus's leadership was essential. He seemed to be the one who could get things done. On his arrival, the directors offered him a salary of £1,000 per year to be general manager of the company. He accepted the job, but refused the pay. "I assure you," he told the directors, "that all the energy and little talent which God has given me shall be bestowed between now and next June

After the failure in 1857, physicist William Thomson spent the winter making improvements. He invented a mirror galvanometer, which could detect signals in a wire at a low voltage. His improvements were key to the success of underwater telegraph cables.

in endeavoring to carry out this enterprise."

Immediately, Cyrus ordered nine hundred nautical miles of new, improved cable. Combined with what was left from last year's supply, and with some recovered cable, he calculated they had a total of three thousand nautical miles. The core was again made of seven copper wires, coated with gutta percha, and protected with iron wire. They applied an improved insulating compound to the new cable. A supervisor at the Gutta Percha Company had invented it so tar wouldn't build up in the wheels of the cable machinery.

Because of last year's failure, Cyrus found it hard to raise more money in England. The company had already lost £100,000, and the public distrusted the whole idea. But he did convince the British government to provide ships again. And, despite the fact that he was impatient to lay the cable in 1858, Cyrus agreed to more testing. William Thomson and other scientists could now do more experiments on how salt water, ocean depth, and water currents affected the cable. And they could learn more about what the ocean floor was like.

Cyrus's experts worked nonstop. William Everett spent six months developing a better paying-out machine. The first one had been built hurriedly, and even Cyrus admitted it was clumsy. Everett's new brake system made it impossible for a brakeman to apply enough force to snap the cable, no matter how rough the sea became. It was much easier to use and took up less space on deck.

Thomson worked all winter to improve the telegraph equipment. He invented a delicate instrument to detect weak electric signals received at the end of a long underwater cable. After attaching a small magnet to a tiny mirror, he hung the mirror by a tight silk thread in the middle of a coil of wire and connected the coil to the cable. He pointed a narrow beam of light at the mirror and its reflection shone on an indicator bar. Even a weak electrical current flowing into the coil caused the magnet and the mirror to turn slightly. This made the spot of light on the bar move to the right or left, one way for a dot, the other for a dash, using Morse code. Thomson called his new invention a mirror galvanometer. Cyrus was amazed at this major improvement in detecting weak signals.

Thomson also worked tirelessly for months to improve the cable design. The quality of the copper in the first cable varied greatly. Thomson still wanted it purer to make the best possible cable, but the company couldn't afford to scrap any left from last year. He insisted on testing each mile of new cable as it was being manufactured.

The trouble was, Thomson's theories caused a problem. Conflict erupted between him and Dr. Whitehouse. Whitehouse insisted on high voltage to create strong pulses at the far end of a long cable. Thomson was convinced high voltage would damage the cable. Besides, his new mirror galvanometer could detect weak pulses, and high voltage wouldn't be necessary. Above all, Cyrus wanted harmony and teamwork, yet he couldn't keep the two men from arguing. Whitehouse seemed stubborn and uncooperative, but he was the company's official electrician, and Cyrus went along with his decisions. More and more, however, Cyrus found he trusted Thomson's ideas.

In March, the USS *Niagara* returned to Plymouth, England, from the Brooklyn Navy Yard. It took 160 men to load the *Niagara* and *Agamemnon* with cable again—3,000 miles of it. Crews worked day and night. Through all of April and part of May, men coiled the cable in the tanks, layer upon layer, until each tank was filled with 200 to 360 miles of cable.

The United States had offered the USS *Susquehanna* as an escort ship again, but in May, Cyrus learned she was quarantined in the West Indies because of a yellow fever outbreak on board. There was not enough time to get another ship from the United States. Cyrus rushed to Great Britain's First Lord of the Admiralty and pleaded for one more escort ship. The country agreed to supply the HMS *Valorous*.

Cyrus worked constantly to ensure success this time, concentrating on all the details. They had improved the equipment and made changes in procedures. Charles Bright, chief engineer, requested that they make a trial trip so the men would be better trained. Cyrus was impatient, but he agreed to allow time for it. This year, ships would start laying cable from mid-ocean, instead of from Ireland. And they planned to leave in June when weather was the best in the North Atlantic. No major storms had occurred in June or July for decades.

USS *Niagara* flew this special flag while laying cable.

Bright led the trial trip, leaving Plymouth on Saturday, May 29, 1858. Both *Agamemnon* and *Niagara* had leftover defective cable on board for the experiments, and Bright brought a dynamometer to monitor and control the strain on the cable while it was being reeled out. The fleet sailed to the northern edge of the Bay of Biscay, west of the English Channel, off the northwest coast of France (47°12' north latitude, 9°32' west longitude), where the water was more than 2,500 fathoms deep. Bright had the crew test equipment and practice all the procedures—splicing cable, retrieving and buoying it, and using the brake on the improved machinery. The success of the upcoming expedition depended on good trial results. Tests went well, and six days later the fleet returned to Plymouth to make a few minor adjustments. Bone-weary, Cyrus caught the next train to London, reported the success of the trial to the company directors, and hurried back to Plymouth. He didn't even have time to sleep, only catching short naps on the train.

Henry Field, Cyrus's youngest brother and a minister, arrived from New York to bless the fleet and was disturbed to find Cyrus looking so haggard. "The strain on the man was more than the strain on the cable, and we were in fear that both would break together," Henry wrote.

The fleet left Plymouth for mid-ocean on June 10. "With the exception of a few of the members of the company and their friends, there were none to bid us farewell," reporter Mullaly wrote.

Of the five ships in the fleet this year, *Niagara* was the only American one. Both cable-laying ships had engineers, electricians, cable splicers, and many crew members. Dr. Whitehouse again declined to sail, and Thomson took his place on the *Agamemnon*.

Cyrus, on board the *Niagara*, felt confident leaving in June, but the mood of the crew was tense. Everyone knew from last year's failure that a split second of trouble could ruin the entire mission. The day was warm and sunny, the sea a brilliant blue. But it was too calm. The crews wanted a breeze so they could use their sails to reach the rendezvous point in mid-ocean, saving their coal supply for the cable-laying process. Instead, they needed to fire up their steam engines to make any headway. On the third day, a breeze came up but soon it became blustery. The wind roared so loudly, men on watch duty had to yell at one another to be heard. The sky blackened, the barometer plummeted, and the sea turned a cold, steel gray.

A fierce storm churned up. Day after day, winds howled and torrential rains drenched everything. The ships lurched back and forth and were tossed around by the violent sea. *Niagara*'s timbers creaked as she rolled in the waves. Cyrus was so seasick, he could barely hang on. The *Niagara* crew watched *Agamemnon* heave up onto the tops of gigantic waves, then

Agamemnon, loaded with tons of cable, almost sinks in a violent storm.

fall out of sight into deep troughs. She leaned so far over, Cyrus wondered whether she could stay afloat. The ships tried to remain within sight of each other, but if they came too close together, they'd surely crash.

After days of being lashed about, the sky began to brighten a little. Cyrus thought the storm was letting up, but then it pounded at them with more force than ever. *Niagara* lost sight of *Agamemnon* and the escort ships as well. Cyrus heard a crack when the *Niagara*'s flying jib boom broke away. Some buoys washed off the deck. The ship was blown more than thirty miles north of where it was supposed to be. Cyrus was shocked when he saw an upside-down lifeboat float by. This was his worst fear. An empty lifeboat meant one of the ships might have gone down and lost all its men.

Finally, after nine grueling days, the storm was over. The *Niagara* had survived, but what about the others? Cyrus saw no sign of them. *Niagara* headed for the rendezvous point, everyone on board scanning the horizon

During the storm, coal breaks loose on the *Agamemnon*, and men are injured when the ship is tossed about.

for signs of sails. Finally, on June 25, the ships met at 51°54' north latitude, 32°33' west longitude, thirty miles east of their planned rendezvous point. Cyrus and the ships' captains had expected to reach mid-ocean four to five days after leaving Plymouth. It had taken more than two weeks.

The ships' lifeboats were put out, and officers started rowing from one ship to another. When Cyrus climbed aboard the *Agamemnon*, he gasped. It was a shambles. Thirty-five tons of coal on the main deck had broken loose and was scattered everywhere. One of the beams had broken. The iron guard at the stern was smashed. Shrouds had come loose, and the captain feared the masts would break. So much water had leaked in, the ship was soaking wet inside and out. The crew reported that "no one expected the cable to hold on from one minute to another." In fact, forty to fifty miles of it spilled out of its tank and slithered across the deck.

Worst of all, the crew was in wretched shape. Cyrus learned that most of the two hundred men had been thrown across the deck by the angry sea pounding against the ship. Many were cut and bruised. One suffered a crushed arm when he was buried under the coal. Men in the galley were scalded when soup sloshed all over them. Four men became caught in the miles of cable that tangled as it spilled. One crewman broke an arm in two places, another broke his leg, and forty-five crewmen were in sick bay. By the time the storm was over, the winds had pushed the *Agamemnon* two hundred miles off course. But Cyrus was relieved that no one had died.

It took several days to make necessary repairs and to recoil the miles of tangled cable on the deck of the *Agamemnon*. At last, sailors rowed the end of *Niagara*'s cable to *Agamemnon*, where cable splicers connected the two ends. They soldered in a sixpence for good luck.

Rain and sleet began to fall. The ships went only three miles before the cable on *Niagara* slipped off the pulley and broke. The crew fired a signal gun and put out a blue light in the predawn darkness to notify the other ships of trouble. Back they came, rowing the end of the cable to the *Agamemnon*, where once again the cables were spliced together. Thomson came aboard *Niagara* to test the ship's equipment. Everything tested well. He returned to the *Agamemnon*, and the two ships resumed laying cable.

After each ship had gone about forty miles, a mysterious break occurred in the electric current. The ships headed back to the rendezvous point again. Cyrus and the *Niagara* electricians rowed to *Agamemnon*, thinking *Agamemnon* caused the break. But *Agamemnon* thought *Niagara* was at fault. Sadly, they determined that the break was miles from either ship, probably on the bottom of the ocean. This was depressing news. Cyrus and Bright and the electricians had no idea what caused it and would not be able to prevent it from happening again.

But Cyrus wasn't beaten. He convinced them to try once more. He told them if the cable broke again before they had gone far, they should return to the rendezvous point and resplice. But if they went more than one hundred miles before a break occurred, they agreed to head for Queenstown, Ireland.

Things worked perfectly for a while. Cyrus began to breathe a little easier. Men kept a constant watch at the paying-out machine. The "old coffee-mill" churned away, and cable reeled out smoothly. Each ship had paid out a bit more than one hundred miles when suddenly, with no warning, *Agamemnon*'s cable broke. It sank to the bottom of the ocean.

Niagara steamed to Ireland. People had feared the fleet was lost in the storm, the worst anyone could remember. Cyrus worried about *Agamemnon*. He had expected the ship to arrive before *Niagara*, because it was laying cable toward Ireland and was closer. After a few days, people became alarmed. They criticized Cyrus for abandoning half of his fleet in mid-ocean. He offered the *Niagara* to search for *Agamemnon*, but it finally appeared. The captain had decided to return to the rendezvous point because they had sailed only a few miles over Cyrus's one-hundred-mile limit. They waited there for days, until supplies became critically low. The men were forced to eat three-year-old salted meat and were almost out of coal. The captain thought they might have to burn masts, spars, booms, and deck planking for fuel if there wasn't wind enough to set sails.

Cyrus now hurried to London to face the board of directors. The news of the failure reached them before he did. This was the second time the project failed, and they had lost a lot of money. Cyrus knew they would be angry. He was right. The chairman wouldn't even come to the meeting. He quit and wrote a letter to the board on July 12, 1858: "I think there is nothing to be done but to dispose of what is left on the best terms we can." He suggested selling the remaining cable and distributing the proceeds to the shareholders. When Cyrus entered the meeting room, he saw that "most of the directors looked blankly in one another's faces." The vice chairman promptly announced he was resigning and stomped out.

Cyrus pleaded with the remaining directors to try again. He told them they had lost only three hundred miles of cable. There was still time. Each ship had more than a thousand miles of cable already loaded. All they needed to do was take on more coal and fresh supplies. Cyrus finally convinced the board of directors to let them try once more. But he was warned if they failed again, the project was finished.

The public was no longer excited. Many thought the attempt was futile. The company's credit fell, and the stock price went way down. But on July 17, 1858, the fleet left once more for the mid-Atlantic. *Niagara* arrived at the rendezvous on July 23. The sailors saw whales spouting, but no cable ship. Cyrus offered a reward to the sailor who first spotted *Agamemnon*. For five days, they climbed rigging and peered through the most powerful telescope, searching for the ship. Several seamen claimed they sighted it in the distance.

Finally, amid patchy fog and mist, one of the sailors cried out, "There she is, sir, on our port quarter." Everyone cheered. *Agamemnon* had hoisted sails to save coal for the cable-laying process and took longer to reach the rendezvous point. Sailors rowed the end of *Niagara*'s cable to the *Agamemnon*. The electricians carefully spliced the cable ends, happy to find that signals were perfect the entire length. They did not insert a lucky sixpence this time.

That day, at the rendezvous, Cyrus wrote in his journal:

> *"Thursday, July twenty-ninth, latitude fifty-two degrees nine minutes north, longitude thirty-two degrees twenty-seven minutes west. Telegraph Fleet all in sight; sea smooth; light wind from S.E. to S.S.E., cloudy. Splice made at one P.M. Signals through the whole length of the cable on board both ships perfect. Depth of water fifteen hundred fathoms."*

He also noted they were 882 nautical miles from the telegraph house at the head of Trinity Bay, Newfoundland.

The ships steamed off in opposite directions as before, slowly at first, testing electrical continuity every ten minutes. And electricians sent a signal to the other ship every time ten miles of cable reeled out.

Agamemnon had to keep cutting out bad sections of cable and resplicing on the deck as it moved along. The electricians decided it must have been damaged during the storm in June.

A whale swam across the stern of the *Agamemnon*, and the men feared it would harm the cable.

Before they had gone far, a huge whale surfaced. Swimming closer, it approached *Agamemnon*'s starboard bow and swam alongside the ship for several minutes. As the startled crew watched, it turned and swam straight across the stern. No one had considered the danger of a whale biting the cable or becoming tangled in it. All aboard stared as the whale grazed the cable, but eventually it swam off without doing any harm.

A short time later, signals stopped suddenly between the two ships, jarring everyone's confidence. An hour and a half later, just as mysteriously as it had stopped, current returned. It was scary not to know what caused these signal breaks. One could occur again at any moment. "We are hourly haunted with a dread that the worst has yet to happen," reporter John Mullaly wrote.

The *Niagara* engineers discovered more cable was reeling out than should be. At that rate, there wouldn't be enough to reach Newfoundland. Realizing the iron protective covering on the cable was affecting the compass needle, they quickly checked their position on the sextant. *Niagara* had sailed sixteen miles off course. If she kept going in that direction, they might have ended up in the Caribbean Sea. Luckily, *Gorgon*, their escort ship, had an accurate compass and could lead the way.

By July 31, each ship had laid about three hundred miles. If the cable broke now, they were doomed. There wouldn't be enough to try again, and they would never have another chance. But by the end of that day, they had reeled out more cable than anyone had ever laid before. Electric current continued to flow through the copper wires, and signals were still good between ships. But how long would their luck last? Men walked along the deck, treading softly, as if their steps might cause trouble. Reporter Mullaly wrote: "We hardly dare ask ourselves if we shall lay the line the whole distance—it seems too much to hope for—and we dread to think of the future. We count the day not by hours, but by minutes."

Cyrus's confidence lifted the crew's spirits. He showed no hesitation outwardly, but his nerves were tight. He found it calming to write precise details, as he always had. Every day, he recorded *Niagara*'s progress, noting the number of miles traveled, the miles of cable reeled out, the water depth, weather, and the distance that *Agamemnon* sailed, each time reports came over the cable. And every journal entry included the mileage to the telegraph station at Bull's Arm, Trinity Bay.

On Friday, July 30, Cyrus calculated they were 793 miles from the telegraph house. The next day, he recorded 656 miles still to go. On Sunday, August 1, there were 511 miles left. Every day they were closer. Maybe they would make it! One sailor wrote in chalk on the outside wall of one of the cable tanks, "The wire will be laid, and we will go to New York."

But on August 2, the fifth day out, electric signals went haywire. Just one kink or rupture in the cable would ruin the entire mission. "We have all become superstitious," Mullaly wrote. It was nearly five hours later when they detected the problem—a defect in the insulation. Luckily, the bad spot was in the cable that was still on board, and the electricians managed to cut out the section and resplice the cable before it reached the paying-out machine. "It was impossible to think of any thing else but the cable," Mullaly wrote.

As more and more cable was laid, Cyrus wrote in his journal, "The *Niagara* getting light, and rolling very much." As usual, Cyrus was seasick. But there were only 357 more miles to the telegraph station.

The next day, August 3, Cyrus recorded that the station was 210 miles away. They spotted icebergs in the distance, floating south from Greenland along the North American coast. Newfoundland was not far off! And, miraculously, *Agamemnon* was keeping pace with *Niagara* as she headed toward Ireland. Signals flowed back and forth between the two ships almost continuously.

On Wednesday, August 4, *Niagara* was just sixty-four miles from the telegraph house at the head of the Bay of Bull's Arm. "Passed several icebergs this morning; made the land off the entrance to Trinity Bay, at 8 A.M.," Cyrus wrote in his journal. Everyone raced to the top deck to see land. Surely they would make it this time. They were so close! Seabirds flew overhead and porpoises jumped playfully in the waves. Cyrus saw countless icebergs, some one hundred feet high, as tall as a ship's mast. He spotted the British steamer *Porcupine*, whose captain came aboard *Niagara* and piloted them into the Bay of Bull's Arm. By that time, it was dark. *Niagara* steamed nine to ten miles to the head of the bay and anchored at 1:45 a.m. on Thursday, August 5.

Cyrus couldn't wait for daylight! He jumped into one of the lifeboats and had a sailor row him to shore. He raced half a mile in the dark, from the sandy beach up to the telegraph house. Out of breath, he banged on the door. No one answered. He ran around to the side of the house, rapped on the windows, and yelled to wake the operators. "The cable is laid!" he shouted. "The cable is laid!"

The station attendants crawled out of bed, shocked. No one had expected the cable to arrive. And amazingly, on the same day that *Niagara* reached Newfoundland, *Agamemnon* anchored close to Valentia Island. Cyrus could scarcely believe his dream had come true. Two thousand fifty nautical miles of electric cable lay across the Atlantic Ocean floor, and current flowed through.

Cyrus was bursting to tell his family and the rest of the world, but it was the middle of the night and the station was closed. The telegraph operator wasn't even there. Cyrus handed two men several messages and insisted they run through the woods to the nearest village, fifteen miles away. Fortunately, landlines to the United States were working. Cyrus's first message was to his wife, Mary. "Arrived here yesterday. All well. The Atlantic telegraph cable successfully laid. Please telegraph me here immediately."

Cyrus sent telegrams to the Associated Press, and right away newspapers spread the news. The *New York Herald* printed Cyrus's announcement: "Trinity Bay, August 7, 1858. The Atlantic telegraph cable was successfully landed here yesterday morning, and is in perfect order. The Agamemnon has landed her end of the cable, and we are now receiving signals from the telegraph house at Valentia."

In a different telegram to the Associated Press, Cyrus wrote, "After the end of the cable is landed and connected with the land line of telegraph, and the Niagara has discharged some cargo belonging to the Telegraph Company, she will go to St. Johns for coal and water, and then proceed at once to New York."

Cyrus also included a message to be sent to President James Buchanan: "Dear Sir—The Atlantic telegraph cable on board the United States frigate Niagara and Her Britan[n]ic Majesty's steamer Agamemnon was joined in mid ocean July 29, and has been successfully laid; and, as soon as the two ends are connected with the land lines, Queen Victoria will send a message to you, and the cable will be kept free until after your reply has been transmitted."

Early the next morning, *Niagara*'s officers and men pulled the tar-covered shore-end cable up the narrow bridle path to the telegraph house. Strong signals came through the underwater cable. Cyrus was so excited, he touched his tongue to it and received "a shock that nearly threw him over."

At the telegraph station in Valentia, Ireland, the cable was turned over to Dr. Whitehouse in perfect working condition.

At Bull's Arm, Newfoundland, ship's officers and sailors pull the cable up the hill to the station, which they name Cyrus Telegraph Station.

"THIS NEWS WILL SEND AN ELECTRIC THRILL THROUGHOUT THE WORLD."

NEW YORK HERALD

"CYRUS THE GREAT"

(1858)

Bells rang from thousands of steeples. Boston fired a one-hundred-gun salute on the Common and shot rockets and fireworks at night. Reporters from St. John, New Brunswick, Canada, wrote: "Bravo, Atlantic Cable! Great rejoicing here for its success." News from Buffalo, New York, announced that "bonfires are blazing on almost every corner, while guns are firing and bells ringing everywhere." In Portland, Maine, "bells rang for half an hour at sunrise, noon and sunset." Hartford, Connecticut, launched balloons. Every city and town in North America seemed electric with excitement—all thirty-two U.S. states and the Canadian colonies.

Henry Wadsworth Longfellow, a well-known American poet, was staying in a hotel near Boston when the news broke on August 5. He entered in his journal, "Standing in the office I hear the click! click! of the telegraph, and presently the clerk says, 'The Atlantic Telegraph is laid!' Soon it buzzes through the corridors, and the whole house is alive with the news." Longfellow sent a letter to a friend, regarding the telegraph. "The great news of the hour, the year, the century," he wrote. "The papers call Field, 'Cyrus the Great.'"

Cyrus telegraphed from Trinity Bay: "Every man on board the Telegraph Fleet, has exerted himself to the utmost to make the expedition successful; and by the blessing of Divine Providence it has succeeded."

The public had expected another failure. Now people hailed the success as "The Great Event of the Age." Some called it "the great triumph of the century." The *New York Herald* announced: "The cable is laid; and now the most honored name in the world is that of Cyrus W. Field."

Letters of congratulation poured in—from friends, from the archbishop of New York, from the bishop of Newfoundland, from Londoners. One letter came to Cyrus's wife, Mary. The moment the family's pastor, Dr. William Adams, learned of the cable's success, he wrote to her. "As your pastor I have known somewhat of your own private griefs and trials, and the sacrifices which you have made for the success of your noble husband. Now the hour of reward and coronation has come for him and for you."

Divine services were held in churches throughout the country. The theme of every sermon was that the cable would bring world peace. In Britain, there was great rejoicing, and on the London Stock Exchange, Atlantic Telegraph Company stock shot up from £340 to £920 per share.

But not everyone rejoiced. "The news of the successful laying of the Atlantic Cable is received here with feelings of suspicion," a Rutland, Vermont, report said. "Very few believe a word of it." A Philadelphia reporter wrote: "It was at first believed to be a hoax—especially so by the wiseacres who prophesied failure from the beginning."

There was so much to do, Cyrus hardly had time to eat or sleep. "The people here seem to have had little faith in the cable's arriving, and had made very slight preparation for receiving it," he wrote to the Associated Press. He alerted the press that electricians needed to unload sending and receiving instruments from the *Niagara*, set them up in the telegraph house, and connect the cable. It would take days, perhaps weeks, to make adjustments. Her Majesty, Queen Victoria, would then send a message, President Buchanan would reply, and the cable would be open to the public.

Queen Victoria sent the first public telegram across the Atlantic Ocean in 1858. This portrait was painted a year later.

After equipment was unloaded, Cyrus placed a telegraph operator, C. V. de Sauty, in charge of the station. He felt confident doing so because de Sauty had supervised the electrical staff on the *Niagara* and things had gone well. Cyrus boarded *Niagara* once more and left for New York, stopping in St. John's to take on coal. While there, a banquet was given, honoring Cyrus. It was particularly meaningful to him, because he knew that the privileges granted to the New York, Newfoundland and London Telegraph Company had aroused criticism. Cyrus told the Executive Council of Newfoundland that he was pleased to hear of the members' approval of the project, which had from the beginning received their "consistent and liberal support."

While he was at St. John's, Cyrus received a telegram from his brother in New York. "Your family is all at Stockbridge, and well. The joyful news arrived there Thursday, and almost overwhelmed your wife. Father rejoiced like a boy. Mother was wild with delight; brothers, sisters—all were overjoyed. Bells were rung; guns fired; children let out of school, shouted, 'the cable is laid'—'the cable is laid.' The village was in a tumult of joy. My dear brother, I congratulate you. God bless you! David Dudley Field."

Niagara was finally ready to steam south to New York. But a persistent fog hung over Newfoundland for five days, delaying departure. Coming out of the harbor, *Niagara* hit a rock, but once Cyrus was assured that damage was minimal and the ship could proceed, he turned his attention back to the cable. Cyrus was worried. He had heard nothing from Trinity Bay for the five days he had been in St. John's. No messages were coming through from Ireland. People began to wonder if the cable did succeed, and if they had celebrated too soon. They waited. Impatient at the delay, people demanded to know when the line would be open to the public. President Buchanan wrote to Cyrus, saying that he had not yet received any message from the queen. Cyrus replied that no one could send anything until instruments were set up. But he was frustrated, and he telegraphed de Sauty at Trinity Bay to find out what was causing the delays.

De Sauty and Dr. Whitehouse in Ireland had sent more than a hundred tests back and forth so they could adjust the cable equipment, but nothing else. De Sauty replied to Cyrus on August 14. "The cause of our not transmitting and receiving intelligence through the cable is that the instruments require a great deal of care and adjusting in getting them ready. I am doing this as fast as possible."

Finally, on August 16, Britain transmitted the first official telegram across the ocean. "Europe and America are united by telegraph. Glory to God in the highest; on earth peace and good will towards men." At last, the cable was working!

Next came the message the world had been waiting for. "The Queen desires to congratulate the President upon the successful completion of this great international work, in which the Queen has taken the deepest interest." Those twenty-five words took more than two hours to transmit.

An interruption followed from Valentia. "Wait repairs to cable." Something was wrong. Queen Victoria's brief telegram was forwarded on to the United States and beyond, assuming it was her entire message. It was so short, many were disappointed. President Buchanan doubted whether it was real. The remaining seventy words from the queen took another fourteen hours to transmit.

> *"The Queen is convinced that the President will join with her in fervently hoping that the Electric Cable which now connects Great Britain with the United States will prove an additional link between the nations whose friendship is founded upon their common interest and reciprocal esteem.*
>
> *The Queen has much pleasure in thus communicating with the President, and renewing to him her wishes for the prosperity of the United States."*

President Buchanan's reply to Queen Victoria included, "May the Atlantic Telegraph under the blessing of Heaven prove to be a bond of perpetual peace and friendship between the kindred nations." His complete 149-word reply took ten hours to reach England.

On August 17, New Yorkers woke up to a tremendous noise. One hundred guns were fired in City Hall Park at daybreak and again at noon. Church bells pealed. Factory whistles blew. Newsboys ran through the dusty streets flailing extra editions of newspapers and shouting the wonderful news! The cable was now working! New York City burst into pandemonium. Bonfires were lit in the streets, businesses closed, and people hung banners in windows and flew American and British flags. Hundreds of workmen creating the new Central Park marched through the streets to the beat of a brass band. Parading along Broadway from Union Square uptown to the new park, they marched close to the Fields' neighborhood. Crowds stood along the shore, looking for the *Niagara*, expecting it to come into view at any moment. Large ships always appeared majestic, but this one was special. *Niagara* had accomplished the event of the ages, and everyone wanted to welcome the ship home. But it didn't arrive.

At dark, one hundred thousand New Yorkers gathered in City Hall Park when fireworks lit up the sky. Things calmed down by 10:00 p.m., but soon after that, a fire broke out on the roof of City Hall, most likely from a spark in the fireworks display a few hours earlier. The bell ringer tried to clang

An extravagant fireworks display celebrating the Atlantic cable's success set New York's City Hall on fire. Before flames could be extinguished, the tower was lost.

the bell at the top of the tower as a fire warning, but flames were so hot, he had to escape. The tower collapsed, and the wooden statue of Justice on top, engulfed in flames, fell into the rotunda of the building.

While New York City was wildly celebrating, Cyrus sat in his cabin on the *Niagara* and wrote a letter to the directors of the Atlantic Telegraph Company.

> *"At your unanimous request, but at a very great personal sacrifice to myself, I accepted the office of General Manager of the Atlantic Telegraph Company, for the sole purpose of doing all in my power to aid you to make the enterprise successful; and as that object has been attained, you will please accept my resignation. It will always afford me pleasure to do any thing in my power, consistent with my duties to my family and my own private affairs, to promote the interests of the Atlantic Telegraph Company."*

The next morning, Wednesday, August 18, the *Niagara* anchored for a few hours, until the tide came in high enough to sail through the Narrows in New York Harbor. Cyrus couldn't wait. He caught a ride to shore on a tugboat and went home, weary and drawn. He had been gone for months. All he wanted was quiet.

But quiet wasn't possible. At 2:00 p.m., the *Niagara* was sighted from the Battery, where at least twenty thousand people were waving wildly. *Niagara*, with flags flying, entered the Narrows. Hundreds of boats hovered around. Bands on board ships played "Hail Columbia" and "God Save the Queen." Signal cannons were fired as *Niagara* steamed up the bay. Staten Island ferryboats thronged with people, clamoring to get close. *Niagara* anchored off the Battery for a while, then proceeded up the East River to the Brooklyn Navy Yard. The captain and officers waved their caps. People cheered "as if they were going mad."

Visitors jammed into rowboats to step aboard the *Niagara*. They wanted to see the cable-laying apparatus and touch the miracle ship for them-

In 1858, composers wrote music to celebrate the success of the transatlantic cable. This cover to the "Atlantic Telegraph Polka" sheet music shows the *Niagara* and the *Agamemnon*, connected by cable, headed in opposite directions to reach North America and Europe.

selves, and a constant stream of men, women, and children trekked up and down the gangways. They marveled at the machinery and peered down into the giant tanks where the cable had been stored. Splotches of tar were all over the ship.

Everyone demanded Cyrus's attention. His brother Henry wrote, "In twenty-four hours his name was on millions of tongues." Praise came from everywhere—President Buchanan, the governor general of Canada, the governor and Legislative Council of Newfoundland, and many other dignitaries. He received honors and medals for this great achievement.

Citizens of western Massachusetts staged a celebration to pay tribute to their local hero.

The popular magazine *Harper's Weekly* featured illustrated news stories about the amazing cable. The City Hall fire appeared on the cover of the August 28 issue. Another week, the magazine published a twelve-stanza poem called "How Cyrus Laid the Cable." On September 4, *Harper's* printed a Telegraph Supplement.

In the midst of all the celebrations and personal honors, Cyrus was worried. From the beginning, he sensed something was wrong with the cable. Between August 10 and September 1, more than 350 technical or government messages crossed between Newfoundland and Ireland, but signals weakened and messages became erratic. Cyrus kept in daily contact with the Newfoundland telegraph station. He had promised that the cable would open to the public after the queen's and president's messages. But it didn't. The official opening kept getting delayed. And the public wanted access.

Access or not, Cyrus and the fantastic cable were on everyone's mind. People wrote music and poems. One song, eleven verses long, was sung to the tune of "Yankee Doodle." It began:

> *"Success, at last, sits like a crown,*
> *Upon our work gigantic;*
> *Behold the Telegraph laid down*
> *Beneath the broad Atlantic.*
> *Yankee doodle, &c . . ."*

Unusual souvenirs were created. Tiffany's, a prominent jewelry company, bought some of the leftover cable, cut it into four-inch segments, and sold the pieces. One company created a perfume, "Atlantic Cable Bouquet," distilled from flowers and ocean spray. A candy maker concocted twisted candy to look like the cable.

Even a new building honored Cyrus. The cornerstone of St. Patrick's Cathedral, a Roman Catholic church, was laid in New York City, and the archbishop included an inscription to Cyrus Field on the parchment in the hollow of the stone.

Cyrus had wanted quiet time at home with his family, but instead was being overwhelmed by all the celebrating. September 1 and 2 were designated International Cable Jubilee days throughout the United States, the Canadas, and Great Britain. The mayor of New York City announced a grand two-day festival. Visitors flocked into the city. They booked every hotel room or found cots and couches anywhere else they could—in attics, public halls, and barrooms. A half million people jammed the streets.

The events on September 1 began at 10 a.m., with services at Trinity Church and a procession of two hundred clergy. Cyrus and the ships' officers received a national salute at Castle Garden, New York State's immigration station, where there was a large auditorium. A four-mile-long parade then inched its way up Broadway to Forty-Second Street, and over to the glass-walled Crystal Palace at Fifth Avenue. New York had staged a world's fair at the palace a few years earlier. Cyrus and the mayor rode in a carriage drawn by six horses. The crowd cheered loudly as they passed by, waving handkerchiefs and tossing hats into the air. A detachment of sixty policemen was followed by cavalry and military regiments. Bands played. A model of the *Niagara*, made on a scale of one inch to a foot, was carried proudly by four sailors. And a remnant of cable from the *Niagara* was coiled and placed on a carriage as part of the parade.

Cyrus saw mottos and banners hanging on buildings all along the parade route. One said, "The Great Event of our Day." Another, "Honor to Cyrus W. Field." An elaborate one depicted two ships laying the cable and included a short rhyme, "Europe from these United States / The sea no longer separates."

Not since the opening of the Erie Canal thirty-three years earlier had New York City celebrated with such enthusiasm. So many people crammed onto one balcony that it collapsed, causing a number of injuries.

The parade was scheduled to reach the Crystal Palace at 4:30 p.m., but the route was packed with crowds and it was almost 6:00 p.m. before it actually arrived. At the palace, the crew of the *Niagara* entered carrying

Crowds cheer as sailors march along Broadway in a four-mile-long parade, carrying a model of the USS *Niagara*.

Ten thousand people filled the Crystal Palace to honor Cyrus and celebrate the success.

models of the *Niagara* and the *Agamemnon*, which they proudly placed in front of the stage, and the ships' captains were honored. The palace was decorated with red, white, and blue bunting, with a large green banner featuring an Irish harp in the center. Cyrus's brother and prominent New York lawyer David Dudley Field was the main speaker. He told the crowd of ten thousand people the story of the cable. It had been four years and three months full of "anxiety and toil." Peter Cooper said the effort took "the far-seeing and electrifying mind of Cyrus W. Field to inspire and stimulate."

A telegram was read that Cyrus received from Ireland that morning when he left the Battery: "The directors are on their way to Valentia to make arrangements for opening the wire to the public. They convey through the cable to you and your fellow-citizens their hearty congratulations in your joyous celebration of the great international work." The

After the Crystal Palace celebration, New York City firemen lead a nighttime procession, including torches and fireworks. Signs and banners decorate buildings, honoring Cyrus and the Atlantic cable.

audience erupted in a tremendous cheer. Following a choral group's singing of Handel's "Hallelujah" chorus, the benediction to close the event was given by Cyrus's father, Reverend Field.

After the festivities, firemen led a torchlight procession back down Sixth Avenue to Broadway. The parade took a detour at Union Square to circle the bronze equestrian statue of George Washington and marched on to City Hall Park for a finale of fabulous fireworks. City Hall looked strange after losing its tower, but a 180-foot-long decoration stretched across the front, with banners of the two cable ships. Above all, in gold letters: "God has been with us: To Him be all the glory."

Joseph Henry, secretary of the Smithsonian Institution and dean of American electricians, commented, "This is a celebration such as the world has never before witnessed."

Cyrus posed for noted photographer Mathew Brady, whose studio was in New York City.

The next evening, September 2, a banquet was held honoring Cyrus and the ships' officers. Six hundred guests and dignitaries arrived at the Metropolitan Hotel in horse-drawn carriages. Fancy centerpieces decorated the tables: flags, ships, images of Queen Victoria, President Buchanan, Cyrus, and coats of arms of all nations. A telegraph machine was set up in the hall to send and receive messages.

The extravagant menu began with oysters on the half shell, relishes, green-turtle soup, or lobster. After that, a choice of eighteen entrées—beef tenderloin, lamb chops, partridge, wild duck, chicken, turtle steak, and more. Dessert included dozens of pastries, fruits, and cakes, as well as ice cream. But Cyrus could hardly eat. Just hours earlier, he had learned from Trinity Bay that signals were weakening rapidly. During the banquet, while speakers were praising him, and six hundred guests were applauding his marvelous accomplishment, he was handed a telegram from Ireland. All he could see was a jumbled note, a broken string of words that meant nothing.

"THE CABLE WAS
LAID, AND FOR FOUR WEEKS
IT WORKED—THOUGH NEVER
VERY BRILLIANTLY."

CYRUS WEST FIELD

"HUMBUG"

(1858–1860)

Electric signals had worked perfectly between the *Niagara* and the *Agamemnon* all across the ocean, and they were clear when the cable ends were connected at both stations. But after a few days, the cable began to have trouble, and the ability to send messages was now crumbling. The question that haunted Cyrus and the electricians was, Why were transmissions getting worse?

Dr. Whitehouse, the company's chief electrician, was stationed in Ireland. He had taken control over the electrical procedures as soon as the cable was connected to the telegraph house. He thought stronger signals were needed. The batteries on board the ships produced 90 volts. Whitehouse added huge induction coils, five feet long, to the sending equipment, and upped the voltage to 2,000 volts. He also replaced Thomson's mirror galvanometer with his own equipment for receiving messages.

Cyrus kept his worries to himself. He did not want the public to know of any problems, but news filtered out. On September 6, the London *Times* published a notice, sent by the secretary of the Atlantic Telegraph Company. "Owing to some cause, at present not ascertained," it read, "there have been no intelligible signals from Newfoundland since 1 o'clock on Friday morning, the 3d." He reported that electricians were investigating the cause, and he concluded, "Under these circumstances no time can at present be named for opening the wire to the public."

By now, everyone's nerves were fraying. Transatlantic messages showed frustration and impatience. "Repeat, please" . . . "How do you receive?" . . . "Send slower." . . . "Can you read this?" . . . "How are signals?" . . . "Please send something."

Cyrus was frantic to know what was wrong. Fortunately, the land line between New York and Newfoundland was functioning, and Cyrus hounded the Trinity Bay telegraph station for information. On September 24, he telegraphed C. V. de Sauty, demanding answers.

Newspapers were becoming more and more important in the daily life of Americans. Printing House Square, close to New York's City Hall, was the home of the *New-York Times*, the *Tribune*, and other papers. Frustrating reports about the telegraph cable appeared in many editions.

"Please give explicit explanations and answers to the following inquiries:—1st—Are you, or have you been within three days, receiving distinct signals from Valentia? 2d— Can you send a message, long or short, to the directors at London? 3d—If you answer no to the above, please tell me if the electrical manifestations have varied essentially since the first of September."

Cyrus W. Field.

De Sauty replied: "TRINITY BAY, Sept. 24.—To Cyrus W. Field, New York:—Have received nothing intelligible since 1st." He ended his reply with, "I cannot send anything to Valentia. Very little variation in electrical manifestations."

Occasionally, a short word or two came across, but rarely a sentence. Newspapers reported discouraging news on one day, hope the next. On September 23, reports came that the cable worked again, then signals were weak on September 27. On and off it went. Men came to Newfoundland from Ireland to try to fix the problems, but that didn't help.

The public now became angry. Accusations spread that the transatlantic cable had never worked at all. Many believed it was one big hoax, including Queen Victoria's and President Buchanan's messages.

But no one paid attention to the fact that important telegrams had crossed the ocean. Messages arrived so quickly they had to have come by cable: it would have taken ten or more days by ship. The British government used the cable twice. One message announced that peace was declared between Britain and China a few days earlier. The other involved a mutiny in India. Britain had sent a ship to Canada with orders for two British regiments stationed there to sail to India at once. Suddenly, the rebellion was over and extra military personnel weren't needed after all. The cable had just been connected, and the British Admiralty immediately sent two telegrams, canceling the orders. The messages arrived in Newfoundland before the regiments left, which saved the troops a long ocean voyage and the British government a lot of expense.

Also, when two Cunard ships collided off the coast of Newfoundland, the cable wasn't yet open for public use. Cyrus let a Cunard company representative send a message, assuring families in England that no lives were lost. At a chamber of commerce meeting in New York, one man jumped up and yelled, "It is all a humbug! No message ever came over!" The Cunard spokesman, who had sent the message and received a reply, stood up, boldly faced the man, and told him he had no right to make that claim.

The transatlantic cable worked for four weeks. Peter Cooper, still the American company's president, said, "We received over it some four hundred messages. Very soon after it started, however, we found it began to fail, and it grew weaker and weaker, until at length it could not be understood any more."

The company directors lost almost $2 million and thousands of miles of cable. Cooper said, "We had been set down as crazy people, spending our money as if it had been water." They also suffered loss of time—precious time. Cyrus and the other company directors knew if they didn't succeed soon, someone else would. Tal Shaffner, one of Cyrus's fierce competitors, claimed the Atlantic cable had never worked, and he planned to connect the continents by a series of short cables, hopping from Scotland to the Faroe Islands, to Iceland, to Greenland, then to Labrador, and Newfoundland. If Shaffner succeeded, Cyrus's company would lose everything. Worst of all, public confidence was zero—just when they needed to raise more money.

In Britain, the Atlantic Telegraph Company fired their electrician, Dr. Whitehouse, both for his incompetence and his refusal to cooperate. He lashed out in a published paper, railing against William Thomson and Cyrus. He blamed the failure on the "frantic fooleries of the Americans in the person of Mr. Cyrus Field."

Cyrus couldn't stop asking himself questions. *What caused the cable to fail? Was it faulty? Was the voltage too high? Was he too impatient?* The cable could have been damaged. There had been a severe lightning storm in Newfoundland soon after the cable came ashore. The cable had been moved back and forth between ship and dockside, twisting, bending, coiling, uncoiling, and recoiling. It could have cracked or been pierced, and seawater could have leaked in and slowly ruined it. No one knew for certain. The electricians and engineers decided if the damaged section was in shallow water, they would try to lift it with a grappling hook and replace it. But they determined the break was far out to sea, in the deepest part of the Atlantic.

Even the officers of the company began to lose faith. "After the failure of 1858 came our darkest days," Cyrus wrote. "It is more difficult to revive an old enterprise than to start a new one. The freshness and novelty are gone, and the feeling of disappointment discourages further effort."

Cyrus was ridiculed. He was scorned. Some said he was nothing but a junk dealer who only sold paper and rags. Ugly rumors sprang up. Being accused of manipulating the stock price hurt him the most. If his accusers had checked his stock sales, they would have known he sold only one share of telegraph stock, at a loss of several hundred dollars. But the public felt betrayed. Cyrus Field plummeted from hero to scoundrel. People avoided him on the streets.

When the cable was considered a success, Newfoundlanders wanted Frederic Gisborne, who introduced Cyrus to the idea, to have part of the credit. But the moment it failed, Cyrus was left standing alone to take the blame. In a flash, success turned into total failure.

Just as Cyrus's dream collapsed, New York City lost its brilliant Crystal Palace. The building where ten thousand people had celebrated the cable's success just a few weeks earlier burst into flames, probably by arson, and collapsed in twenty-one minutes.

No clear messages had come through the cable since the banquet on September 2, but confused signals continued to plague the telegraph operators for several more weeks. The *New-York Times* later reported that "the whole thing was voted a humbug" and "the great success was a great fizzle."

"There was a profound discouragement. Many had lost before, and were not willing to throw more money into the sea," Cyrus said. The financial panic of 1857 led to a severe economic depression in the United States, which continued to worry potential investors. But Cyrus refused to give up. He knew the cable had worked. He had nearly been electrocuted by it!

Cyrus left for Europe again in May 1859 to request British government support for a renewed cable attempt. His timing couldn't have been worse. The Atlantic cable wasn't the only failure. An attempt to lay a cable in the Red Sea and over to India had just failed, and the British government was suffering from an overwhelming financial loss. On June 8, Cyrus met with the Atlantic Telegraph Company directors for the first time in many months. They were reluctant, but Cyrus persuaded them to try again and to raise £600,000 to lay a new cable. Britain finally agreed to provide government funds if—and only if—it worked. They didn't intend to lose any more money and refused to fund any further major cables until the failures were investigated.

More than eleven thousand miles of cable had been laid around the world, but only three thousand miles of it were functioning. The British government's Board of Trade ordered a thorough investigation of underwater telegraph cables. In July, a committee of inquiry was formed with eight members, four from the Board of Trade and four specialists from the Atlantic Telegraph Company.

Cyrus would have to wait while scientists conducted elaborate experiments. While they investigated cable construction and insulation. While they tested sending and receiving instruments, and speed of signaling. While they studied how pressure and water depth affected a cable. Equipment was made to test the quality of copper and insulating substances. In fact, Cyrus figured the committee examined every single thing about manufacturing telegraph cables and laying them. He could do nothing to hurry the process. The committee listened to dozens of presentations from scientists, engineers, oceanographers, manufacturers, and electricians, including several by William Thomson.

Home for the Christmas holiday, Cyrus hoped to spend the closing days of 1859 with his family. He had just turned forty and had spent little time with his wife, Mary, and their five children. But once again, family life was interrupted. Just after Cyrus W. Field & Company paid back stockholders from the 1857 panic, a fire broke out in a building next door. Cyrus rushed to the site and found his office and a warehouse collapsing in flames. His total inventory was a pile of ashes. Immediately, he convinced a friendly competitor to let him borrow space to set up a temporary office. The very next day, he placed a notice in the *New-York Commercial Advertiser*, listing an address "where our business will be carried on as usual."

While Cyrus worked to revive his paper company and waited fretfully for the results of the Board of Trade's inquiry, the United States geared up for a presidential election. In late February 1860, a candidate from Illinois arrived in New York City to campaign. Cyrus's brother David escorted Abraham Lincoln to the platform at Cooper Union, where Lincoln spoke to a large audience. For decades, arguments had been brewing over slavery. Lincoln was resolute about stopping the expansion of slavery, and he thrilled the New York public. Many shifted their support from the leading candidate, New York senator William Seward, to Lincoln. Cyrus continued to support Seward. He had been an immense help getting cable support through the U.S. Senate and was a loyal friend.

In 1860, Abraham Lincoln came to New York City, campaigning for the U.S. presidency. He had not yet grown a beard.

Cyrus and his family embarked on a two-day excursion aboard the enormous luxury liner *Great Eastern* when it came to New York City in 1860.

In July, Cyrus learned that the biggest ship afloat, the SS *Great Eastern*, would steam into New York City. The ship's builder, Isambard Brunel, had shown him the luxury liner when it was under construction in London years earlier and Cyrus wanted to see again how enormous it was. He bought tickets for his family and friends to embark on a two-day cruise to

Cape May, New Jersey, and back. Called "The Wonder of the Seas," the ship was hard to control and crashed into the New York pier. The Fields found the cruise sickening—a filthy ship with wormy food, and half the waiters were drunk. Cyrus was so disgusted, he and his party disembarked and chartered a small steamer to return to New York.

Cyrus remained as determined as ever to lay a successful transatlantic cable. But by early December 1860, another financial panic swept the country. People wouldn't even talk with him about a cable, much less invest in one. And his paper company suffered its third total loss in twenty years. His creditors accepted payment of 25 cents on the dollar. Still, Cyrus wouldn't give up. He "placed a mortgage upon everything he owned, including the portraits of his father and mother," his daughter wrote. The mortgage included his house and furnishings, his stock in both the New York, Newfoundland and London Telegraph Company and the Atlantic Telegraph Company—even his pew in the Madison Square Presbyterian Church.

In November, Abraham Lincoln had been elected president, and on December 20, 1860, South Carolina seceded from the nation. Six days later, a small Union garrison moved into Fort Sumter in Charleston Harbor. Trouble was brewing.

"I NEVER WORKED SO
HARD IN ALL MY LIFE."

CYRUS WEST FIELD

WAR

(1861–1865)

By February 1, 1861, six states had joined South Carolina in secession. On February 4, a peace conference met in Washington, D.C., to discuss ways to prevent more states from seceding. More than 120 delegates gathered, including Cyrus's brother David. But it was too late. On the first day of the peace conference, Confederate states met in Montgomery, Alabama, to declare themselves an independent nation. A month later, Abraham Lincoln was inaugurated. He refused to acknowledge the Southern states as a separate country. War seemed inevitable.

Cyrus was concerned for the country and about how to revive his paper company. But he was consumed by the Atlantic cable, becoming more and more restless, waiting for the report from the British Board of Trade. In April, after almost two years, the committee announced its initial findings. The members noted haste in pushing the project forward and the use of high voltage as causes of the 1858 cable's failure. But Cyrus was excited to learn that the report said an improved transatlantic cable would work. He thought he could finally move ahead with his plans to revive interest and raise money to replace the cable that failed. But he couldn't. Investors in the United States weren't interested in a cable; they were focused on war.

On April 12, Confederate forces fired on Fort Sumter, capturing it the next day. President Lincoln called for seventy-five thousand volunteers to enlist in the Union military forces. Telegraph operators clicked his message quickly, and thousands rushed to the call. Cyrus's two sons, Edward and Cyrus William, whom they called Willie, were too young to enlist. But Cyrus's nephew Heman, Matthew's son, volunteered. He had been working in Cyrus's paper company. Military units were organized quickly, and Heman practiced drilling in Central Park. On April 19, he marched proudly down Broadway in the Seventh Regiment, the first New York regiment to go to war. Another nephew, Henry, joined a Massachusetts regiment.

A month after the war began, Queen Victoria declared Great Britain's neutrality. To President Lincoln, her proclamation meant that Great Britain was recognizing the Confederacy as an independent nation, which he still refused to do. Lincoln knew the South was Britain's major supplier of cotton, and to keep its textile mills running, Britain had to trade with the Confederacy. Lincoln did not trust Britain to stay neutral. When Cyrus learned that thousands of British troops had been sent to Canada to guard the border with the Union, he became more worried. He needed Britain's cooperation to lay a transatlantic cable.

President Lincoln instituted a Revenue Act in August of 1861, which taxed people with annual incomes over $800, to help pay for the war. Cyrus realized the costs of war would severely hinder his efforts to raise funds.

The telegraph was of critical importance to President Lincoln during the Civil War. Cyrus knew the president visited the telegraph office at the War Department several times a day. It was located right across the lawn from the White House, and he could walk there easily. Portable telegraph units were moved along with the troops and set up near battlefields. So Lincoln was able to communicate with his Union generals wherever they were and click off orders right from the telegraph machine.

Cyrus thought he could help. Early in the war, he wrote to the assistant secretary of war, recommending that the Union connect headquarters in Washington, D.C., with Union forts along the coast by underwater telegraph. He spent weeks traveling back and forth between New York and

Thousands of miles of telegraph wire were strung near battlefields during the Civil War. President Lincoln could communicate directly with his military officers.

Washington, D.C., meeting with his friend William Seward, now secretary of state, and General George McClellan.

In August, Cyrus was torn away from talks in Washington in order to serve as a pallbearer at his mother's funeral in Stockbridge, Massachusetts. Everyone in town heard the church bell toll seventy-eight times, the number of years of her life. After the funeral, Cyrus rushed back to Washington, D.C., to resume discussing coastal cables. His idea met with little success, but eventually the War Department bought fifty miles of the leftover unused Atlantic cable from 1858 and laid some of it across Chesapeake Bay, the rest in the James River from Jamestown Island to Fort Powhatan.

The war caused Cyrus other concerns. The American Telegraph Company, which he, Peter Cooper, and others had founded, lost half of its

Portable telegraph stations, such as this tent, were set up wherever troops camped.

stations the moment the country split in two—those on the East Coast south of Maryland and in the Gulf states. Western Union was continuing to expand and would likely pick them up. In October of 1861, Western Union completed a telegraph line all the way to the Pacific Ocean. Stephen, Cyrus's brother who was chief justice of California, sent the first transcontinental telegram. Cyrus and Mary's children were excited that "Uncle Judge" could send a message three thousand miles, from San Francisco to President Lincoln in Washington, D.C. But they were not excited that their father spent all his attention on two thousand miles of underwater cable. Occasionally, they griped, "Oh, if that old cable was only at the

When the USS *San Jacinto* captured Confederate diplomats from the British ship *Trent*, it brought the United States and Great Britain to the brink of war. The incident sparked renewed interest in a transatlantic cable.

bottom of the ocean!" To which Cyrus always replied, "That is just where I wish it to be."

Cyrus was having trouble convincing anyone that a transatlantic telegraph cable would be worth the investment, when suddenly the Union found itself in a serious predicament. On November 8, 1861, the USS *San Jacinto* intercepted the British mail steamship *Trent* in international waters off the coast of Cuba. Two Confederate diplomats and their aides were seized from the *Trent*, brought back to the United States, and imprisoned in Boston. When the British government learned about it two and a half weeks later, they were outraged! Britain was officially a neutral country, and it was a violation of international law to stop and board a ship of any neutral country in international waters. Britain demanded the men's immediate release, plus an apology from the U.S. It took so long for Britain's ultimatum to reach President Lincoln and learn his response that

Britain had time to plan attacks against the Union. The British government sent eight thousand additional troops to Canada. War seemed close at hand. Reluctantly, Lincoln released the captives. "We had one big war on hand and we didn't want two at the same time," he said. The London *Times* reported that Britain almost declared war with the Union because there was no telegraph cable across the ocean.

Cyrus jumped into action. "Now is the time," he wrote to the Atlantic Telegraph Company in London, "to act with energy and decision."

He sent a letter to Secretary of State Seward in Washington, D.C. "The importance of the early completion of the Atlantic telegraph can hardly be estimated," he wrote. "A few short messages between the two governments and all would have been satisfactorily explained."

In January 1862, Secretary Seward wrote to Charles Adams, the U.S. ambassador to Great Britain, that President Lincoln was willing to cooperate with Britain in laying a successful transatlantic cable. Cyrus sailed to London with renewed hope of gaining support, but he found it difficult. Unlike Cyrus, many influential Londoners sympathized with the South. Even though he disagreed with them politically, he maintained friendships. He hosted elaborate parties for business, government, and social leaders to promote a new Atlantic cable, and while people listened with interest, he couldn't persuade many to invest in his project.

Cyrus's many trips between New York and London caused some people to believe he was secretly investing in deals with the British to support the Confederacy. Someone who never signed his name wrote letters to ruin Cyrus's reputation and, in February, a London newspaper printed one. In March, Cyrus was startled to read in the London news that he had been indicted for treason in the United States. Quickly, he booked passage back to New York. When he arrived, he spent only two hours with his family before he raced to Washington to ask about the indictment. He learned he had been charged with "treasonable proceedings with the public enemy." Obviously, someone had intentions of harming him, or his cable project. He couldn't find out who it was. The grand jury withdrew the indictment, but Cyrus continued to receive threatening letters, presumably because of his many British connections. He wrote to an American friend in London: "I regret exceedingly to find a most bitter feeling in this country against England."

But Cyrus was stubborn. That summer, he tried desperately to raise money in the Union states for another cable expedition, traveling from one city to another. "It was inspiring to hear him talk," his brother Henry commented. When Cyrus spoke in Boston, "they applauded the projected telegraph across the ocean as one of the grandest enterprises ever undertaken by man." But after the meeting, Cyrus wrote: "I did not get a solitary subscriber! In New York City I did better, though money came by the hardest effort."

In October 1862, Cyrus left for England again. Britain's attitude toward the Union was shifting. Two events had eased feelings. A bloody battle at Antietam in September blocked the Confederate army's advance into the North, causing Britain to believe the Union might be able to win the war. And Lincoln announced a few days later, on September 22, that he would free all slaves in the Confederacy on January 1, 1863. Britain now felt the Union was fighting to end slavery, a practice that the British Empire had abolished thirty years earlier.

Cyrus resumed his hectic schedule of dinners and meetings. Despite a more cooperative atmosphere, trying to raise money in England for the transatlantic cable remained tough. And with war raging at home, he worried about his family. How he wished the transatlantic cable had worked, so he could contact his wife at a moment's notice.

He wrote his four daughters, Mary Grace, Alice, Isabella, and Fanny, on November 22, 1862: "I have been very anxious to get through and leave here so as to be with you on Christmas." But that wasn't possible. Without Cyrus's inspiration and leadership, things didn't seem to get done. He told his daughters, "Be very kind to your blessed mother, and do everything in your power to make her happy. I have purchased *all* the things that you gave me a memorandum of, or have written me about. Good-bye, my dear children, and may God bless you all. With much love to your mother, Eddie, and Willie, and kind regards to all the servants."

Lincoln stands with officers at Antietam. After the battle, the British began to think the Union could win the war, which helped soften the difficult relations between the two countries.

In December, Cyrus endured fifteen seasick days on a stormy crossing, arriving home three days after Lincoln signed the Emancipation Proclamation. A few weeks later, Cyrus wrote to the directors in London: "The whole country is in such a state of excitement in regard to the war that it is almost impossible to get any one to talk for a single moment about telegraph matters." But he assured them he would continue to do everything he could to raise money for a new cable.

It still wasn't easy. People with money avoided him. "Some days I have worked from before eight in the morning until after ten at night to obtain subscriptions to the Atlantic Telegraph Company," he wrote.

Cyrus's trips wore him out, but he forced himself to keep going. In one two-week period, he traveled more than 1,500 miles, visiting major cities along the Atlantic coast and as far west as Buffalo, New York. Sometimes he went by train, other times by stagecoach. He tried to persuade audiences that experts were sure an improved cable would work, but he couldn't raise much money. A few weeks later, he sailed back to England, where he met often with the Atlantic Telegraph Company directors. The secretary reported, "Mr. Field has crossed the Atlantic twenty-five times on behalf of the great enterprise to which he has vowed himself. He has labored more than any other individual in this important cause."

In July 1863, the British government's Board of Trade published final results of its investigation, in a report longer than the Bible. It summarized the reasons for earlier failures, in addition to specifying how to make and lay improved cable. Cyrus focused on the positive sections. He read that a carefully made, well-insulated cable could be laid and "may reasonably be relied upon to continue for many years." It was just what Cyrus wanted to hear!

He wasted no time. While he began to collect proposals to manufacture an improved cable, fierce fighting at Gettysburg, Pennsylvania, resulted in a Union victory. But thousands of soldiers were killed. News of the battle didn't reach England until two weeks after it was over.

Several days later, news came of a draft riot in New York City. Hundreds of men had set fire to the draft office, and a riot continued for four days until Union soldiers finally stopped it. Cyrus opened a letter from David's wife. The family had been terrified. "As the rioters approached our house they were met by a company of soldiers," she wrote. *Were Mary and the children safe?* Cyrus wondered. They lived next door to David. How he wished a cable lay across the ocean so he could send a telegram.

As quickly as he could, Cyrus finished his immediate business in London and returned home. On November 11, 1863, an article on the front page of the *New-York Times* caught his eye: "The Atlantic telegraph cable is certainly to be tried again. It appears that the indefatigable Mr. Cyrus Field has just come over from England to New-York, bringing a specimen of the new cable."

New draft laws were put into place in 1863. Men had to join the army or pay $300 each. Hundreds of laborers in New York City became enraged and began rioting. The mob came dangerously close to Cyrus Field's home in Gramercy Park.

But another problem blocked Cyrus's efforts. President Lincoln no longer seemed to support his transatlantic plan. Lincoln wanted telegraph access to Europe, but he was now more interested in a Western Union plan to run a telegraph line from San Francisco, north through British Columbia, landlines through Russian America, and wires across Siberia to St. Petersburg, Russia. That plan would require only a short underwater cable across the Bering Strait, even though it meant thousands of miles of landline. People assumed Cyrus's Atlantic cable would fail: Western Union's plan seemed more likely to succeed.

Cyrus didn't intend to be beaten. He had persisted with his transatlantic plan for years and knew it would work. Nothing was going to stop him now. His cable would bring nations together, but he must hurry.

In mid-January 1864, Cyrus headed back to England. "The Atlantic Telegraph project is again attracting public attention," reported *The Telegraphic Journal*, published in London. "Mr. Cyrus W. Field (one of the leading spirits of the undertaking) is again amongst us, full of hope, and ready to embark once more in the gigantic enterprise."

Cyrus hadn't been able to raise much money in the United States and now desperately needed British support. One day in February, he met one of the wealthiest men in the world, Thomas Brassey, a London financier. Brassey owned the world's largest railroad company, employing more than eighty thousand people. "I went to see him, though with fear and trembling," Cyrus said. "He received me kindly, but put me through such an examination as I never had before. I thought I was in the witness box." Cyrus came out of the meeting with a smile on his face. He had just convinced Brassey to invest in the project, with "a pledge of sixty thousand pounds sterling!" John Pender, a member of the House of Commons, equaled that amount. Their generous support inspired others to contribute.

The new cable would be a better quality than the one used in 1858, based on findings from the Board of Trade's extensive inquiry. And it would have much better insulation. The problem was that it would be thicker—and heavier. It wouldn't even fit into two ships this time. *How could they lay it?* Cyrus wondered. He needed a miracle.

Daniel Gooch, chairman of Britain's Great Western Railway, contacted Cyrus with a deal. He and Brassey had just bought the *Great Eastern*, the ship Cyrus had seen in London during its construction, and the one he and his family had sailed on briefly out of New York. This "Wonder of the Seas" had failed as a luxury liner, and they purchased it for a fraction of its cost. It was the only ship in the world that could carry enough cable to cross the

The enormous *Great Eastern* was the only ship in the world that could carry enough cable to cross the Atlantic. Cyrus could scarcely believe he could use it.

ocean. The Atlantic Telegraph Company could use the ship to lay a cable across the Atlantic—at no charge. If the project was a success, the owners wanted stock in the cable company. *No charge?* Cyrus could hardly keep from jumping up and down. This was the miracle he had been looking for. "In all my business experience I have never known an offer more honorable," he wrote.

He rushed to the cable manufacturer. About that time, Glass, Elliot and Gutta Percha Company merged, becoming the Telegraph Construction and Maintenance Company. Cyrus asked if the firm could make 2,300 nautical miles of cable by spring of 1865. A deal was made.

Cyrus had another task. In July of 1864, he sailed to Newfoundland to select a place to land the new Atlantic cable. *Great Eastern* was too large to steam all the way to the head of the narrow bay where *Niagara* had landed in 1858. He found the perfect spot, calm but deep enough for *Great Eastern* to anchor close by—a tiny fishing village on Trinity Bay named Heart's Content. Cyrus walked along the shore, confident that he would land a cable there next summer.

"FOR A WEEK
ALL WENT WELL."

CYRUS WEST FIELD

"THE WONDER OF THE SEAS"

(1865)

Cyrus felt sure the transatlantic telegraph would finally succeed. The British were manufacturing new cable, they were supplying the ideal ship, and they were pouring their money into the project. Cyrus had arranged for James Anderson, one of Cunard Lines' best captains, to command the *Great Eastern*. And Heart's Content, Newfoundland, was the perfect spot to land the cable.

Wanting his own country to be part of the endeavor as in 1858, Cyrus headed for Washington, D.C., in March of 1865, carrying letters. He and Peter Cooper and the other honorary officers of the Atlantic Telegraph Company were requesting that President Lincoln release a Navy ship to help escort the *Great Eastern*. Cyrus could usually persuade people to embrace his ideas, but not this time. Lincoln left the decision up to the secretary of the Navy, who absolutely refused. He couldn't spare a warship and, like Lincoln, didn't want to cooperate with Britain. There was nothing Cyrus could do.

Elaborate paying-out machinery was placed on the aft deck of the *Great Eastern*. The machinery was much larger than that built for laying the cable in 1857 and 1858.

A few days later, he left for England to make final preparations for the expedition. The moment he arrived, he went to see the *Great Eastern*, anchored at Sheerness, by the mouth of the Thames River. By far the biggest ship in the world, she could carry five times more cargo than the *Niagara* could. One-eighth of a mile long, she had two enormous boilers, two gigantic paddle wheels, a propeller, and six masts, with more than an acre of canvas sail. Some folks claimed that a ghost haunted the ship, but no one could prove it.

The ship was undergoing major changes. On the top deck, at the stern, Cyrus saw the complex paying-out machinery with its grooved wheels. Engineers and mechanics would watch day and night to make sure the cable kept on its track. A brakeman would stand on duty at the dynamometer to regulate tension. A small steam engine, called a donkey engine, was placed in the bow to run a pick-up machine. The machine would reel the cable back in if they had to cut out a faulty section. One deck below,

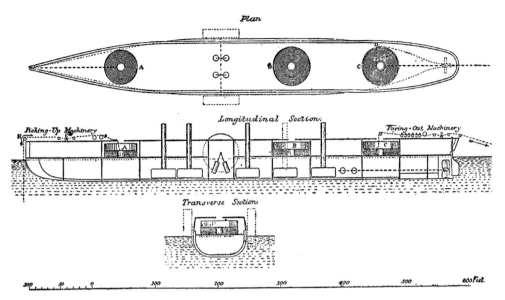

One level below the open deck on the *Great Eastern*, cable was coiled into three huge tanks: one near the bow, one midships, and the third at the stern. One of the ship's five boilers and its smokestack had to be removed to make room for the tanks.

the fancy staterooms and ballroom had been gutted out, and in their place, workers were scurrying to finish building supports and foundations for the three huge round tanks that would hold the cable. One tank was placed in the bow, one midships, and the third aft, near the stern, each more than twenty feet tall. If workers had tried to coil all the cable into one stack, it would have been sixty feet high—and so heavy, the cable near the top would have squashed the bottom layers.

Two British steamships, HMS *Terrible* and HMS *Sphinx*, were assigned to escort *Great Eastern* to America. *Sphinx* would carry sounding equipment to measure ocean depth along the route so the paying-out crew would know how much slack to allow. Where the water was deep or where there were steep underwater drop-offs, more slack would be needed to ease the strain on the cable as it reeled off the ship.

Cyrus checked in at the cable manufacturer. He had ordered 2,300 nautical miles of cable, to have lots of extra. The cable had a new design: Pure copper wire was used. It was better insulated. And it had an improved protective layer. Larger than the 1858 cable, it was more than an inch thick, and the shore end was thicker than that. The new cable was much heavier, weighing a ton and a half per mile. Factory workers had been laboring day and night for six months. Cyrus insisted that it be ready in two more months. They would make it, if all went well.

There was another problem: the water wasn't deep enough for the *Great Eastern* to be docked alongside the cable factory in Greenwich. The ship was anchored thirty miles down the Thames River at Sheerness. Two old ships took turns transporting cable sections to the big ship. As soon as a several-hundred-ton section of cable came out of the factory, it was loaded onto one ship and towed downriver, while the other was being loaded. At Sheerness, the cable was coiled into the tanks on the *Great Eastern*. The end of each section was spliced to the cable already coiled. All three tanks

Small ships were loaded with cable as it was manufactured, then sent downriver to Sheerness, by the mouth of the Thames River. Here a ship transfers cable to the *Great Eastern*.

were filled, making one long continuous cable, which the electricians tested constantly.

While Cyrus was concentrating on cable details, America's Civil War finally came to an end. The news did not reach England until a week or so later. Cyrus was elated, until he learned the following week that President Lincoln had been assassinated just days after the Union victory. When Cyrus learned of Lincoln's death, he told his British friends, "Just before leaving America I called to see President Lincoln, and I know how deeply he desired peace in America and peace in all the world." Cyrus also learned that his good friend William Seward, Lincoln's secretary of state, was attacked at the same time and had been seriously wounded. How Cyrus dreamed of peace! And he believed that a transatlantic cable would help bring it.

Preparations for the expedition were proceeding well. On May 24, Queen Victoria's son Albert Edward, Prince of Wales, paid a visit to the ship. Almost two thousand miles of cable had been loaded. Cyrus showed Prince Albert the room where the telegraph apparatus was kept and invited him to send a test message. Electricians connected one end of the cable to the sending apparatus and the other end to the receiving equipment. Prince Albert had them send, "I WISH SUCCESS TO THE ATLANTIC CABLE." The message came out the receiving end in less than a minute. Everyone cheered.

Cyrus wrote a letter to his brother Henry and sent it on the next ship leaving for New York. "We have now over 2200 nautical miles of cable completed, and expect to sail the last of June, or early in July. All is going on well. With love to your wife. I remain, Your affectionate brother, Cyrus W. Field."

Once the cable was all coiled on board, the *Great Eastern* took on the remaining provisions for the voyage—tons of coal, and supplies, such as buoys and clamps, and five miles of strong wire rope to lower the cable overboard in a storm if necessary. The crew stowed a few multipronged grappling hooks on deck. They loaded tons of food for more than five hundred men. Boxes and barrels were hefted on board. A milk cow was led up

Men carefully coil the cable inside one of the iron tanks.

the gangplank, along with sheep and pigs, plus crates of turkeys and other birds. Each day the butcher would kill what they needed.

On July 15, the *Great Eastern* was finally ready. Samuel Canning, the chief engineer, had been with Cyrus from the beginning, since crossing Cabot Strait with high society passengers and Newfoundland dogs. C. V. de Sauty, who had managed the cable station at Bull's Arm, Newfoundland, was the ship's electrician, and William Thomson and others came along to assist in any necessary electrical work. William Russell, a London *Times* correspondent, was on board to record the event, along with two artists. Cyrus was the only American on the ship.

At noon, Captain Anderson ordered the anchor raised. Nearly two hundred sailors pushed the capstan round and round to lift the seven-ton anchor. The anchor chain alone was monstrous, each link weighing seventy pounds. Finally, the massive ship steamed out of Sheerness, loaded with seven thousand tons of cable. HMS *Porcupine* guided it out into the English Channel. Cyrus knew the *Porcupine*—the ship that piloted the

Niagara into Trinity Bay in 1858. Maybe it would bring good luck. People stood along the shore to catch a glimpse of the wondrous *Great Eastern* as it passed the cliffs of Dover and steamed on through the channel, headed for Ireland.

The steamship HMS *Caroline* followed behind, struggling to keep up in a stiff wind. She was loaded with the heavy shore-end cable, to be attached to the telegraph station at Foilhummerum Bay, a small cove near the southwestern tip of Valentia Island. Crowds gathered there, and people pitched tents atop the cliff to wait for the ships. No one wanted to miss this event.

People couldn't see the *Great Eastern*, anchored far offshore. But they spied the *Caroline* coming in. More than twenty small boats rowed out to meet her. Eager to help, the sailors made their boats into a pontoon bridge to carry the end of the cable close to the beach. When they reached the shallow water, people splashed through the surf and grabbed the cable. They hauled it onto the sandy beach, up the steep cliff, and across a field to the telegraph house, where electricians attached it to the apparatus on a table inside. The crowd cheered loudly, and Sir Peter FitzGerald, the Knight of Kerry, bid everyone good luck. He said this was the "greatest undertaking of modern times."

The *Caroline* headed for the *Great Eastern*, reeling out the heavy shore-end cable. She passed the Skellig Islands, two gigantic chunks of rock jutting out of the ocean. When she met the *Great Eastern*, men care-

The 1865 cable was more than an inch thick. It had seven copper conducting wires in the center, surrounded by insulating and protective layers.

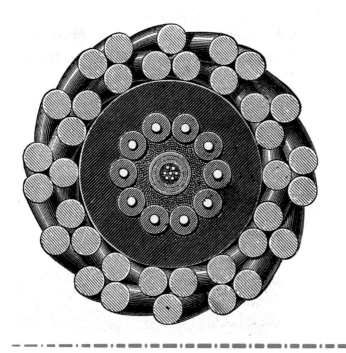

The shore end of the 1865 cable was thicker than the deep-sea cable because it needed more protection.

fully spliced the shore end to the long cable. Cyrus watched them strip each protective layer back, solder the wires, then rewind the layers. The electric current was perfect. They were ready to go!

On Sunday, July 23, 1865, *Great Eastern*'s "huge paddles began to revolve slowly," the propeller started spinning, and the great ship inched forward toward North America. Cyrus felt sure everything would work this time. He could scarcely breathe, he was so excited. At last, his dream would come true. The machinery rumbled in a steady rhythm, winding the cable around the grooved wheels, over the stern wheel, and into the blue-gray sea.

Cyrus did not have a specific job on the ship, but he kept abreast of every detail. He often stepped into the dark testing room, where Thomson and the other electricians were watching the tiny light on the mirror galvanometer, hardly blinking their eyes, lest they miss a clue.

Samuel Canning, in charge of the expedition, ran a tight ship. Every task was organized. Rules were carefully spelled out, and there were lots of them. The first thirty minutes of each hour, the electricians tested insu-

Large buoys and grappling hooks are stored on deck in case they are needed.

lation, and the next half hour was divided into three 10-minute periods to send and receive signals from the telegraph house in Ireland. They couldn't do both at the same time: while insulation was being tested, there was no way for the ship to communicate with shore. Every fifty nautical miles, they reported their distance. If they lost continuity in the line, someone was assigned to bang the gong just outside the testing room door, and Captain Anderson would stop the ship.

Things went well—at first. But before they had gone eighty miles, the gong sounded. A break in electrical continuity was the culprit. Cyrus paced the deck, frustrated. Canning alerted him that they must remove a section that had already been reeled out. Canning then ordered the cable to be brought to the pick-up machine in the bow. Not an easy task.

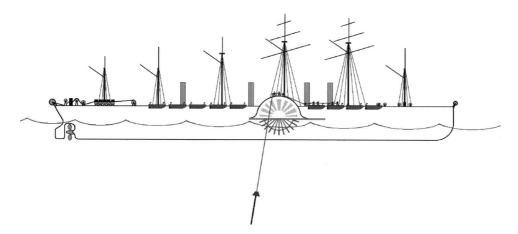

After mechanics cut and clamped the cable, sailors pulled the wire rope and cable from the stern of the *Great Eastern* to the bow, where they would feed it into the pick-up machine. Once the cable was repaired, the captain would continue west toward Newfoundland, laying cable once more.

— ▬ ▪ ▬ ▬ ▪ ▬ ▬ ▪ ▬ ▬ ▪ ▬ ▬ ▪ ▬ ▬ ▪ ▬ ▬ ▪ ▬ ▬ ▪ ▬ ▬ ▪ ▬ ▬ ▪ ▬ ▬ ▪ ▬ — ▪ —

The mechanics quickly clamped the cable to a long wire rope. After cutting the cable above the clamp, they let it drop deep into the water with the clamp and the rope attached. Captain Anderson turned the ship around until it was in line with the cable already laid, pointing toward Ireland. Dozens of sailors grabbed the end of the wire rope and pulled it through the water. Trudging along one side of the ship, they lugged the cable forward the entire length—one-eighth of a mile, from the stern to the bow. They had to maneuver past the machinery, around lifeboats and deck equipment, and over the top of a paddle wheel to feed the cable into the pick-up machine in the bow. The *Great Eastern* steamed forward very slowly while the pick-up machine reeled in the cable. The little donkey engine "puffed and wheezed as if it had the asthma." Hours later, after reeling in ten miles of cable, they spotted a tiny flake of iron that had pierced through the insulation, causing seawater to seep in and ruin the signal. The electricians cut out the damaged section. Sailors trudged back to the stern clutching the end of the slimy cable, where electricians spliced it to the cable at the paying-out machine. The whole process was so tedious and cumbersome,

When a damaged section of cable was detected, men reeled it back in and inspected every inch to determine the problem. The tedious procedure took many hours.

it was enough to fray anyone's nerves. Cyrus figured they lost thirty-seven hours because of a tiny piece of metal.

After that, things went smoothly for a while—until the cable flew off the drum and caught in the wheels. They cut and spliced again, causing further delay. It seemed as if anything could go wrong at any moment and ruin the entire project.

And no one could depend on the weather. Heavy seas whipped up into a gale, and the *Sphinx* fell behind in a strong headwind. She disappeared— and she was the only ship with sounding equipment. The captain couldn't turn *Great Eastern* around to search. It was all he could do to keep a steady pace to reel out the cable.

All the men feared they would hear the gong at any moment. Sometimes they hardly dared to breathe. And some of them were panicked by the ghost. The sailors claimed it was real—and alive! Lying on their bunks, they found it almost impossible to sleep at night. They heard moaning and groaning and something kept scratching on the iron walls of the hull. Legend had it that a riveter had fallen into the double hull while building the ship, and he'd been in there screaming ever since.

One good thing: Because of its size, *Great Eastern* rode the waves easily. Cyrus had crossed the Atlantic at least thirty times, and this was the first time he had not been seasick.

Three hundred miles from Ireland, the weather was fine, and signals were good. Cyrus sent a message to the Valentia telegraph station, "We expect to reach Heart's Content August 5th."

The crew members did manage to have some fun. Henry O'Neil, one of the artists, printed a humorous ship's newspaper every few days named *The Atlantic Telegraph*. He drew sketches and reported silly news, like the port side of the ship was moving faster than the starboard, probably because the pigs were on the starboard side, weighing it down. The August 2 issue included the chorus to a song the coilers made up to chant as they worked, round and round, uncoiling cable all day. It began:

> *Copper and zinc! acid and stink!*
> *tink-a-tank-tink-a-tank-tint-a-tank-tink.*

Still, they listened for the dreaded gong. On July 29, the seventh day out, when they had laid about eight hundred miles of cable, it sounded again.

"Pass the cable forward to the 'pick-up,'" Canning ordered abruptly.

The crew lugged the cable forward, as before. The water was two miles deep, instead of only three-fifths of a mile, as it was the first time. They had to pull harder to overcome the weight of more hanging cable. The donkey engine chugged away, pulling in the slimy cable, until the men spotted another thin piece of iron sticking out, just like the first one. Everyone clustered around while the electricians cut out the faulty section. Maybe this was not an accident. "No man who saw it could doubt that the wire had been driven in by a skilful hand," reporter Russell wrote.

Cyrus had heard that saboteurs sometimes ruined the cable of a competing company. He did have fierce competitors, and someone had recently

This drawing, printed in the *Great Eastern*'s newspaper, shows Cyrus sitting in the cable tank. He and others took turns guarding against sabotage.

tried to ruin his reputation. *Who could have done this?* he wondered. Soon he and Canning realized the crew on duty in the tanks was the same crew that had been on duty when the first damaged piece of cable was detected. Canning hated to do it, but he exchanged those men for a different crew. Cyrus and a few other men volunteered to take turns standing guard in the tank.

O'Neil sketched a skinny Cyrus on duty for the last issue of the ship's newspaper. He called it *The Night-Watch* and wrote a ditty below it:

> *No useless sentry within the Tank*
> *Not in slumber or sleep we found him*
> *But he sat like a warrior stiff on his plank*
> *With his Inverness cloak around him*

On August 2, Cyrus sat on watch duty when a loud scraping noise startled him. A workman saw a sharp flake of iron sticking into the cable exactly like the other two pieces. Cyrus had been watching carefully. If someone was sabotaging their effort, surely he would have seen him. The breaks weren't caused by a traitor, but by the cable itself! Bits of brittle sheathing had flaked off. Cyrus hollered to the lookout man, but the message didn't reach the deck in time to stop the machine. The faulty section of cable reeled out over the stern.

The ship was about six hundred miles from Newfoundland, and Canning again ordered the cable to be brought forward to cut the bad section out.

A strong wind picked up, shifting from one direction to another. The captain couldn't hold the ship still, and the cable chafed against the hull. As the pick-up machine reeled the damaged cable onto the deck, the tension became so great, it snapped.

"Stop it!"

"Look out!"

Before the men could grab the cable, it slid across the deck. The cable sank two and a half miles into the sea.

"It's all over—it is gone," Canning cried, hurrying to his cabin.

Cyrus's face turned an ashen white. His lips quivered. But he took a deep breath and said to the men in a calm, controlled voice, "The Cable has parted and has gone overboard."

They had laid a little more than 1,200 miles of cable when it was lost. Maybe there was a ghost on this ship, ruining their effort.

"No words could describe the bitterness of the disappointment," Russell wrote. "The Cable gone! gone for ever down in that fearful depth! It was enough to move one to tears."

Fortunately, they knew exactly where it went down, because it slipped away a few minutes after noon, and they had just taken a perfect observation with the sextant.

Cyrus knew the telegraph operators in Ireland would be worried. No one had notified them that the cable was being cut to make a splice, and signals must have stopped abruptly. The last the operators knew was that

Great Eastern was six hundred miles from Newfoundland, hoping to land in a few days.

Canning decided to grapple for the lost cable. They couldn't take soundings to find out how much line to drop because the *Sphinx* was long since gone. And some thought the grappling hooks might break the cable. But Canning insisted on trying. The crew attached the hook to the wire rope, which was made in sections with an iron swivel placed at every five hundred to six hundred feet, so it wouldn't twist too much. But a heavy wind churned the ocean into a white froth. The crew placed a buoy so they could tell where to find the spot when the sea became calm.

After the wind died down, they lowered the hook to the ocean floor and dragged it across the path of the cable. When they snagged something, they slowly reeled in the rope. Three of the four times they grappled, they hooked the cable, and the men held their breath. But each time, before they could bring it to the surface, the grappling rope broke. The cable, some of the rope, and the hook sank. But the cable did *not* break! Cyrus clung to the fact that the cable was strong enough to survive attempts to lift it to the surface from the deepest part of the Atlantic Ocean.

One time, the men shouted, "We have caught it! we have caught it!" Everyone jumped. But the line came up empty. Another time, a wheel broke and the rope whipped around the deck, gashing two men in the face.

The weather turned foggy. The *Great Eastern* and the *Terrible* blew their fog whistles every twenty minutes to let each other know their locations. When the fog lifted, the *Great Eastern* had drifted more than thirty miles from where the cable sank. Heavy rains and high winds plagued them for days. The blacksmiths worked frantically at their forge on deck, making new grappling hooks and swivels. But they ran out of wire rope, and Canning had to give up. They left buoys to mark the spot.

Captain Anderson signaled the *Terrible* to go to St. John's. Cyrus had hoped to be in Newfoundland himself in a few days, landing a telegraph cable. He was weary, and worried. His family might not even know he was alive. Before the ships parted, Cyrus gave the *Terrible* a letter to take to Newfoundland and asked that it be telegraphed to his wife from there. He

The crew sets out a buoy to mark the spot where the cable was lost.

wanted Mary to know what had happened as soon as possible. As usual, his letter focused only on the facts. "*Great Eastern* left mouth of the Thames July 15th. Shore end landed in Ireland on 22d. Parted on August 2d in latitude 51° 25' north, longitude 39° 6' west, 1062.4 miles from Valentia Bay, 606.6 miles from Heart's Content. Spent nine days in grappling; used up all wire, rope; nothing left, so obliged to return to England. Three times cable was caught, and hauled up for more than three-quarters of a mile from bed of the ocean."

Terrible flashed its signal lights. "Farewell."

"Good-bye, thank you," *Great Eastern* replied.

The ships headed in opposite directions. Russell wrote, "There was a profound silence on board the Big Ship."

On the way back to Ireland, Cyrus stayed up nights writing plans for next year. They had almost succeeded, and he remained hopeful, but he was nervous about presenting another failure to the directors.

London newspapers reported on August 7 that there had been no news from the *Great Eastern* for four days. The next week, newspapers all over America reported no word from the ship. A Portland, Maine, paper stated that a ship had seen one of *Great Eastern*'s buoys floating in the water. News finally came that the *Sphinx* had arrived safely in Newfoundland.

When *Great Eastern* reached Ireland, a newsman came running. "We thought you went down," he exclaimed.

The *New-York Times* headlines on August 16, 1865, read, "THE CABLE LOST." The news item read, "The failure of the great Atlantic cable is at length confirmed." The report concluded, "As the parting took place where the water is about 14,000 feet deep, there is little probability that the cable can ever be recovered."

The public wasn't surprised. They had expected the cable to fail. It seemed so unlikely to succeed, Western Union had construction crews working on the overland lines to connect to Europe by way of Siberia. But Newfoundlanders had remained hopeful and gathered in Heart's Content, waiting for the fleet to arrive. When the *St. John's Daily News* finally reported that it wouldn't be coming after all, the crowd left, frustrated and disappointed.

Cyrus still wouldn't give up. He persuaded the Atlantic Telegraph Company directors to try one more time. He could use the *Great Eastern* again, so he ordered more cable, then went home. On his return voyage to America, he told a fellow passenger, "We've learned a great deal, and next summer we'll lay the cable without a doubt."

"IT HAS BEEN A LONG,
HARD STRUGGLE."

CYRUS WEST FIELD

"THE CABLE IS LAID"

(1866)

October 1865 was special for the Field family. Cyrus and Mary's daughter Isabella was being married, and Cyrus made certain to be home. He hoped to stay through Christmas, but in November he received a letter from Captain Anderson in England. "I am sorry you are not here. Somehow no one seems to push when you are absent," he wrote.

Anderson's letter disturbed Cyrus. There was still money to be raised, more changes to be made to the *Great Eastern* and to the cable—hundreds of details. Hurriedly, he packed his traveling bags.

When he arrived in England on Christmas Eve, he discovered the company he thought he had left in fair shape suddenly was at a standstill. Even worse, the directors had returned all the money people had just invested in the project.

Cyrus was horrified.

The directors told him they learned the Atlantic Telegraph Company had no legal right to sell additional stock because it had been established by an act of Parliament. Approval was required to sell more shares, and Parliament wasn't in session.

When would it be? Cyrus wanted to know.

Not for several months.

There was no time to wait for Parliament. Cyrus *had* to lay the cable this summer. Western Union was moving ahead with the landline to join North America to Europe through Russia, and if Cyrus didn't succeed soon, everything would be lost. "This was a terrible blow," he wrote.

Immediately, he approached Brassey, Gooch, and Pender, his staunchest supporters. They had an idea. Create a new company. They incorporated the Anglo-American Telegraph Company in March. Each of them, plus seven others including Cyrus, invested £10,000, the cable manufacturer added £100,000, and "in fourteen days we had raised the whole £600,000," Cyrus wrote. The company started immediately to manufacture more cable and load the ship.

While returning from mid-ocean last year, Canning and Cyrus had written out goals and developed a bold plan. They would lay not only one cable, but two! After they laid the new one, they would go back and lift the broken end of last year's cable, splice it to leftover cable, and lay it the rest of the way to Newfoundland.

Cyrus pushed everyone to move quickly. Blacksmiths forged better grappling hooks, and mechanics made stronger rope of hemp and forty-nine strands of wire—about two inches thick. It wouldn't break this time! Instead of last year's wheezing little donkey engine, they installed a 70-horsepower engine in the stern so Captain Anderson wouldn't have to turn the gigantic ship around to reel in faulty cable.

The *Great Eastern* required work. Men attached an iron cage over the propeller to keep the cable from getting tangled. Captain Anderson and his crew figured out a way to reduce drag and use less coal. For weeks, they scraped the underside of the hull while the ship was anchored, removing a two-foot-thick crust of barnacles and mussels with strings of seaweed dangling.

The electricians created a better technique for testing and signaling. Last year, while insulation tests were being run, there was no way to communicate with the station in Ireland. Now they would be able to do both at the same time.

Improvements were made to the cable, although they planned to use what was left from last year. The new cable was the same size, but it was being manufactured with galvanized iron wires in the protective layer. The hope was that no pieces would flake off! The factory raced to crank out the cable at twenty miles a day to meet Cyrus's deadline of finishing and loading by June.

More changes. The route for 1866 was slightly different—thirty nautical miles south of last year's route—so when they went back to grapple for the old line, they wouldn't snag the new one instead.

Finally, Cyrus and Canning weren't taking any chances that someone working in the tanks could purposely damage the cable. "The cable-watch are clothed this expedition in canvass dresses which fit over their ordinary clothing," wrote John Deane, secretary of the Anglo-American Telegraph Company. The outfits were fastened from the back and had no pockets, and the men wore slippers. Boots or shoes had nails in them and were not allowed.

Samuel Canning was in charge of the expedition again. Willoughby Smith, chief electrician of the cable manufacturing company, supervised the electrical department. Others joining Cyrus on the trip included William Thomson, Daniel Gooch, and artist Robert Dudley.

Every single minute was accounted for, and there would be no nonsense. According to Cyrus, "Everything was perfectly organized to the minutest detail." Canning made sure that all rules were clear to everyone. Instructions and diagrams were written out for both ship and shore. The electricians kept an eye on the clock for Rule 11: "Ship will reverse the currents every fifteen minutes, in addition to this, ship will send four reversals of two minutes each, commencing at the thirtieth minute of each hour."

Rule 29 read, "Once a day ship will send distance run, miles paid out, and insulation resistance per mile." The list was long.

Finally, on Saturday, June 30, they were ready. Cyrus walked up the gangplank. *Great Eastern* weighed anchor from Sheerness. Captain Anderson couldn't load all the coal they needed until he reached deeper water. Heavily loaded, the big ship almost grounded on a sandbar. Once she made it into the English Channel, things went well.

The fleet was all British. The small steamship *William Cory* carried thirty miles of shore-end cable to be reeled out from Valentia. HMS *Terrible* led the fleet, and the SS *Albany* and SS *Medway* steamed alongside *Great Eastern*. They would help drag up last year's cable. The shore-end cable for Heart's Content was loaded onto *Medway*, plus seven hundred miles of leftover cable to connect to last year's cable once they lifted it.

The weather turned miserable, spitting hail at them, with heavy winds. Again this year, Cyrus was the only American on the expedition. On July 4, on their way to Ireland, Captain Anderson raised the American flag to honor the ninetieth anniversary of the independence of the United States.

They loaded supplies and livestock in Ireland. Cyrus, compulsive list maker that he was, checked off the live animals: 10 bullocks, 114 sheep, 20 pigs, 29 geese, 14 turkeys, plus hundreds of ducks and chickens, including 18,000 eggs.

Foilhummerum Bay, Valentia Island, July 7. The crew connected about forty boats to make a pontoon bridge. The shore-end cable weighed eight tons per mile, but a gang of men managed to lug one end of it up the cliff to the telegraph house. Signal tests were perfect, and the *William Cory* reeled it out and buoyed it in water one hundred fathoms deep. There were no celebrations or speeches. The public didn't seem to have much faith anymore in the project.

Skeptics shook their heads. It was bad luck to leave on Friday the thirteenth. And the day was miserable—foggy, with a heavy rain falling. The *Great Eastern* crew may have wondered if the ship's ghost was laughing at them. Would it cause trouble again this year? But Captain Anderson was ready to go. And Cyrus certainly was!

Many men were needed to lug the shore-end cable through the shallow water and up the cliff to the telegraph house at Foilhummerum Bay, Valentia Island.

Captain Anderson found the buoy that the *William Cory* had left, and the electricians spliced the shore end to the cable on board. Cyrus watched closely while they tested for electric signals. Perfect. The fleet was on its way—1,686 nautical miles from Valentia Island to Heart's Content.

The second day out, a sailor from the *Terrible* fell overboard. Instantly, a crew member threw him a line and pulled him back aboard, frightened but unhurt.

The pesky cable kinked and twisted from time to time, but otherwise things went according to plan. Signals to and from the Valentia station were good. It felt eerie, things went so well. Except for the weather. "We had fogs and storms almost the whole way," Cyrus noted.

Finally, after two weeks at sea, they heard gulls and saw porpoises and icebergs. Land was near!

The *Great Eastern* laying cable. The ship steamed through rough seas most of the way across the Atlantic.

Cyrus became more and more anxious. He sent a message to Richard Glass, who was in charge at Valentia, to ask how long it would take after landing the cable before the public could use it. Cyrus didn't want frustrating delays like they had eight years ago.

"If you land the cable on Friday," Glass replied, "I see no reason why it should not be open on Saturday."

Exactly what Cyrus wanted to hear!

As they neared the Newfoundland coast, Cyrus kept an eye out for the coastline. But he couldn't see it. "Here we are now [6 a.m.] within 10 miles of Hearts Content, and we can scarcely see more than a ship's length," Deane wrote in his diary on Friday, July 27.

Sailors hoisted the ship's flags. Suddenly, the sun came out. Never had Newfoundland looked so glorious!

"We sent the end of the cable to the *Medway* to be spliced. I left the *Great Eastern* in a small boat at 8:15 A. M., and landed at Heart's Content at 9 o'clock," Cyrus wrote.

Fewer people showed up in the little village this year, but flags of Britain and the United States flew in the breeze, welcoming the fleet. Men dug a trench for the cable. *Medway* laid the shore end as close to the beach as she could. They coiled the rest onto a flat-bottomed boat and hauled it ashore.

Visitors began streaming into town from all around the countryside to see the spectacle. They came on foot, on horseback, in wagons, and in boats.

"There was the wildest excitement I have ever witnessed. All seemed mad with joy, jumping into the water and shouting as though they wished the sound to be heard in Washington," Daniel Gooch wrote in his diary.

Cyrus, on the other hand, was furious. They had come all the way from Ireland, and the short cable across Cabot Strait wasn't working! No one had expected success, so they hadn't bothered to fix it. Cyrus demanded that it be repaired at once. "Is there a steamer," he asked, "to be had in these waters?"

"The Bloodhound is at St. John's," came the answer.

"Telegraph instantly to charter her to go around to the Gulf of St. Lawrence, and fish up the old cable and repair it." Immediately, Cyrus ordered another ship to deliver telegrams across the gulf until the cable was working again.

Cyrus sent the first telegram to his family. "Heart's Content, July 27.—We arrived here at nine o'clock this morning. All well. Thank God, the cable is laid, and is in perfect working order." Mary and the rest of the family learned the good news on Sunday, July 29, after church. Cyrus also sent dispatches to the Associated Press, announcing the fleet's arrival and praising the crew.

On July 27, Queen Victoria's message transmitted easily: "to the President of the United States, Washington.—The Queen congratulates the President on the successful completion of an undertaking which she

Queen Victoria's message was sent through this telegraph station in Valentia.

hopes may serve as an additional bond of union between the United States and England." Her message took just a few minutes to send, instead of the sixteen hours it had taken in 1858.

President Andrew Johnson responded to the queen with a similar sentiment.

Several telegraphers who had sailed on the *Great Eastern* had been assigned to stay and operate the station at Heart's Content. The first day, fifty messages were sent, at a speed eighty times faster than the 1858 cable.

But Cyrus wasn't finished. He had one more task to accomplish, the hardest of all—complete the laying of last year's cable. Most people thought the idea was crazy. Lifting it would be impossible, and it wouldn't work anyway. Cyrus paid no attention. He and Canning directed the crews to transfer six hundred miles of 1865 cable from *Medway* to *Great Eastern*, now that the big ship had room in its cable tanks. Electricians could measure how far from shore the break was, but Cyrus was glad they had taken observations just before they lost the cable and knew exactly where to find it. While *Great Eastern* was taking on more coal, the *Albany* and the *Terrible* went ahead to locate the buoys and start grappling. *Great Eastern* and *Medway* left Heart's Content on August 9, headed straight for latitude 51°25' north, longitude 39°6' west.

The buoys were gone. The *Terrible* skirted north to check but found no trace of them. It was difficult to take new observations because the weather didn't cooperate. As soon as they could use the sextant and find the spot, they hoped for a fairly calm sea. But most of the time, a hefty wind blew, causing heavy swells. When the *Great Eastern* arrived, Captain Anderson steered the ship fifteen miles east of where the broken end of the cable should be.

Canning had the plan worked out. They released the heavy wire rope, and the hook splashed into the ocean, taking two hours to reach the bottom. The first drag didn't work, and it took another two hours to reel the rope back in. The next day, they snagged the cable and started lifting it. Everyone on deck watched in silence. After hours of slowly reeling in the rope, it dropped. The swivels clanked and scraped against the take-up reel. Heavy waves rocked the ship.

Nasty weather slowed progress, but whenever it improved enough, Canning ordered a grappling hook to be dropped. Several times they snagged the cable. One night, they brought the cable partway up, and decided to buoy it until daylight. But the rope slipped and fell to the bottom. Another time, when the hook came up, some prongs were badly bent, which meant they probably caught a rock. And in the rough water, a buoy broke loose from the ship and bumped against one of the paddle wheels.

"Still we worked on day after day. Once, on August 17th, we got the cable up," Cyrus wrote, "and had it in full sight for five minutes, a long, slimy monster, fresh from the ooze of the ocean's bed." But just as they were ready to reel it in and onto the deck, the cable slipped back into the water.

Cyrus and Canning thought they had brought plenty of grappling rope, but each time they grappled, they lost some of it. For weeks they tried. Twenty-nine times they dropped a hook, but they failed to bring the cable

Recovering buoys is a dangerous task.

to the surface. Canning couldn't make many more attempts. They were running low on equipment.

Canning decided there was just enough rope to try once more if they could move to shallower water. On August 31, he ordered Captain Anderson to move eighty miles still farther east, where the ocean wasn't so deep. They dropped another grappling line, and they could tell the cable was hooked when the dynamometer showed increased strain. The take-up machine started reeling in the line, slowly—very slowly. Everyone stood still, not daring to move. Cyrus watched the tension gauge rise as the cable came up. When it was halfway to the surface, Canning ordered the men to connect a buoy to the rope. Then he had Captain Anderson move the ship a couple of miles west toward the loose end of the cable. He hooked it again and raised it partway up.

Canning sent *Medway* another few miles west, to raise the cable close to the surface and try to break it by speeding up the take-up machine with a jerk. They would lose miles of cable from the loose end, but breaking

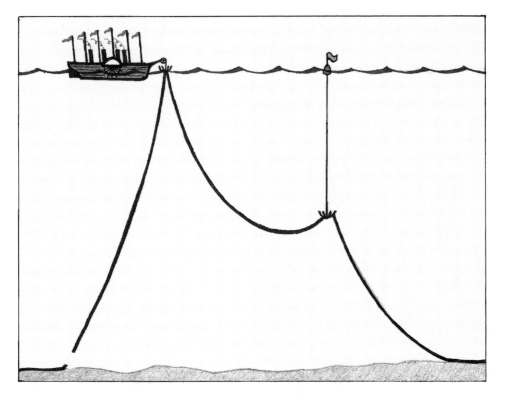

In the final attempt to raise the 1865 cable, Samuel Canning ordered it to be buoyed when it was partway up. After the *Medway* snagged it a few miles to the west and broke it to further reduce the tension, the *Great Eastern* could reel in the cable.

it would relieve the strain, so *Great Eastern* could pull in the cable that was connected to Ireland. *Medway* succeeded, and the tension on *Great Eastern*'s rope was dramatically reduced.

Up came the cable, slowly. In the darkness, with light flickering from the ship's lanterns, everyone watched the grappling rope rise. Canning ordered two men to be lowered on ropes to grab the slimy cable when it surfaced and secure it to other ropes. They didn't want it to slip away again. Crew members lowered lifeboats, in case one of the men fell into the water. At last, before dawn on September 2, the cable came aboard. "It was only when the cable was brought over the bow and on to the deck that men dared to breathe," Cyrus wrote.

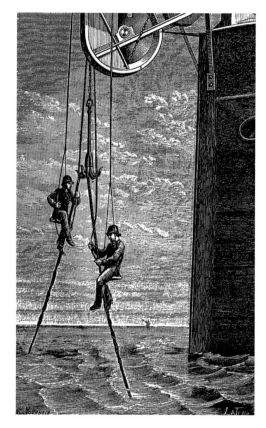

Two men are lowered over the bow of the *Great Eastern*. They are attaching ropes to the cable to be certain they won't lose it.

Cyrus helped tug the slippery cable to the testing room. The electricians stripped it bare, wiped it off, connected it to the testing device, and sent a message to the station at Valentia. "Canning to Glass. – I have much pleasure in speaking to you through the 1865 cable. Just going to make splice."

They waited. *Would anyone see their message?* Cyrus checked his watch.

One minute. Two minutes. Five minutes. Nothing.

Ten minutes. Fifteen minutes.

Wait! The light beam was moving! Valentia heard them!

"Understand, Query."

The testing room nearly exploded with the shrieks of the men. Every man on the ship began cheering. The ship fired guns and rockets. "The roaring bravos of our guns drowned the huzzas of the crew, and the whiz of rockets was heard rushing high into the clear morning sky to greet our consort-ships with the glad intelligence," Robert Dudley wrote.

Cyrus couldn't wait to tell his wife. Mary had supported him for years without complaint, and he wanted her to be the first to know. He sent his first message to her. "The cable of 1865 was recovered early this morning, and we are now in perfect telegraphic communication with Valentia, and on our way back to Heart's Content, where we expect to arrive next Saturday. God be praised." If all the cables were working, his message

After attaching the end of the 1865 cable to the ship's telegraph equipment, electricians sent a message to Valentia. Here, they wait, watching closely for a reply. Cyrus, seated at the left, holds a watch in his hand, which he checked every few seconds.

would travel farther than any telegram had ever traveled before—from the deck of the *Great Eastern* in the middle of the ocean to Ireland, then to Newfoundland, and on to New York—more than four thousand miles.

Electricians spliced last year's cable to the leftover cable on deck and started laying it. The fleet headed back to Newfoundland in a wild storm that dropped soaking rains and blew high winds at them for three days. Cyrus worried about the cable reeling off the stern.

He had one burning question. The electricians sent his message to Valentia: were the cable they had just laid across the Atlantic and the new one across Cabot Strait in working order?

The answer came back, "Both O. K."

On September 7, 1866, after recovering the 1865 cable, Cyrus sent a telegram to his brother Henry in New York, telling him they were getting close to Heart's Content and hoped to land the second cable the next day. He asked Henry to tell his wife, Mary, and brother David Dudley. The message traveled from the *Great Eastern* to Ireland, then across the Atlantic Ocean to Newfoundland by the cable they had laid a few weeks earlier.

"Never shall I forget that eventful moment," Cyrus wrote. "I went to my cabin, I locked the door; I could no longer restrain my tears—crying like a child, and full of gratitude to God."

On September 2, a telegram was sent from Heart's Content to newspapers in the United States. "The Atlantic cable of last year was picked up this morning at 4.40 o'clock, in latitude 51.52, longitude 36.03."

In the midst of a storm, *Great Eastern* cut through the waves. The light beam on the receiving equipment moved back and forth. Cyrus was called

People cheer heartily and lift the heroes in chairs to celebrate the arrival of the second cable in Heart's Content, Newfoundland.

into the testing room to receive a message. It came from Mary, sending prayers and good wishes. "This was like a whisper of God from the sea, bidding me keep heart and hope," he wrote.

A few days later, they reached Newfoundland. Cyrus watched the sailors. "They dragged the shore end up the beach at Heart's Content, hugging it in their brawny arms," he wrote. "Brave, stalwart men they were."

Cyrus's big dream finally came true. "It has been a long, hard struggle," Cyrus said to the New York Chamber of Commerce, "nearly thirteen years of anxious watching and ceaseless toil. Often my heart has been ready to sink. Many times, when wandering in the forests of Newfoundland, in the pelting rain, or on the deck of ships, on dark, stormy nights—alone, far from home—I have almost accused myself of madness and folly to sacrifice the peace of my family, and all the hopes of life, for what might prove after all but a dream."

Cyrus Field had endured disappointment and failure and had met overwhelming obstacles, clinging to his dream of connecting Europe and North America by underwater cable. With relentless drive, he had gathered around him the most experienced people he could, motivating them to work together. From his first meeting with Frederic Gisborne to this final success, he had devoted a fortune and more than twelve years to his dream. He could say at last, "Thank God, the cable is laid."

EPILOGUE

Cyrus Field was not yet forty-seven years old when the two successful transatlantic cables were laid in 1866. The achievement was so spectacular, Peter Cooper called it "the wonder of the world." Queen Victoria honored the Englishmen involved. Some were knighted, others made barons. Cyrus wasn't a British subject, but British newspapers quickly dubbed him "Lord Cable." The United States awarded him a Congressional Gold Medal, and he received many other awards and recognitions from all over the world.

In November of 1866, the New York Chamber of Commerce held a banquet in Cyrus's honor at the Metropolitan Hotel, the same place where crowds celebrated just before the 1858 cable failed. A telegraph instrument was again set up in the room. Instead of one jumbled note coming through the wires, congratulatory telegrams poured in from dignitaries in the United States, Canada, and England.

The Atlantic cable failed after a few years, but it was repaired and later replaced. Many more transoceanic cables were laid throughout the world, several by the *Great Eastern*. The science took off like lightning. The first cables could transmit about seven words per minute. By the 1950s, 2,500 words per minute could be sent, transmitting in both directions at once. Telegraph companies competed, merged, and changed management for decades.

Heart's Content operated its cable station until December 31, 1965, almost one hundred years after Cyrus Field landed the 1866 cable. The telegraph station was named a Provincial Historic Site in 1974. During Cyrus Field's time, Newfoundland was a colony. In 1949, Newfoundland plus all of Labrador became Canada's tenth province, and in 2001, its official name became Newfoundland and Labrador.

Work on the Russian America line stopped abruptly as soon as workers learned of the success of the transatlantic cable, but it was eventually

Cyrus Field, standing beside his globe and holding a piece of cable, poses for photographer Charles DeForest Fredricks.

completed. In 1867, the United States purchased Russian America and renamed it Alaska. The territory became the forty-ninth state in 1959.

Telegraph cables played an important role in world communication for more than a century. Eventually, radio, telephone cables, satellites, fiber-optic cables, and wireless networks made telegraph cables obsolete. Cyrus Field would be amazed to see people in the twenty-first century using cell phones and computers, communicating by word or image anywhere in the world at the tap of a finger or by voice recognition. The investigation committee created by Great Britain's Board of Trade in 1859 to study submarine cables pushed the process of scientific testing to new levels. This played a major role in developing the new science of electricity and magnetism, and in setting standards and processes of research and development in other fields of science.

After the success of the transatlantic cable, Cyrus Field became deeply involved in the expansion of New York City's elevated railways. A generous benefactor, he donated to many causes, including the fund for the base of the Statue of Liberty. He contributed generously to his hometown of Stockbridge, Massachusetts. In his later years, Cyrus was betrayed by Wall Street financiers whom he thought he could trust, and he lost another fortune.

Cyrus and Mary Field celebrated their fiftieth wedding anniversary in 1890. Mary died the following year, and their oldest daughter, Mary Grace, died a few months later. Their son Edward and daughters Alice, Isabella, and Fanny lived for several more years. Isabella wrote a book about her famous father. Cyrus and Mary's youngest child, Cyrus William, died of consumption (tuberculosis) in his thirties, two years after his father. Cyrus died at his summer home, in Ardsley, north of New York City on the Hudson River, on July 12, 1892. He was seventy-two years old.

His tombstone reads:

CYRUS WEST FIELD
TO WHOSE COURAGE ENERGY AND PERSEVERANCE
THE WORLD OWES THE ATLANTIC TELEGRAPH

Cyrus Field was a courageous, persistent, risk taker with lofty ideals. His loyal comrade and able commander, Sir James Anderson, wrote to him in 1879, more than a decade after their expeditions on the *Great Eastern*: "To have been the pioneer *par excellence* in this great work should be most gratifying to yourself and your family, and no one can take from you this proud position."

AUTHOR'S NOTE

Ideas are sometimes wrapped in strange packages. When I was writing *Captain Mac*, my biography of Arctic explorer Donald MacMillan, I took a trip to Newfoundland and Labrador. The icebergs fascinated me, as did the rugged terrain and its hospitable people, but it was a tour of Heart's Content Cable Station Provincial Historic Site that captured my imagination.

A native Mainer, I have always been drawn to the Atlantic Ocean. When I stand on the rocky coast and gaze out, it usually looks calm. But it's eerie being in the middle of the huge ocean, with nothing but water on the horizon for days and days. My first trip to Europe many years ago was by ship, larger than the *Niagara*, but much smaller than the *Great Eastern*. We encountered a hurricane on the way home, making many passengers sick and causing a delay in our arrival in New York. When I read how Cyrus Field steamed across the Atlantic dozens of times to lay the transatlantic cable, I wondered, *Why would anyone do that?*

Then came the research. I found Cyrus Field to be a fascinating character, one who persevered through more trials and ordeals in the dozen years he spent trying to connect the continents than most people face in a lifetime. My research, while captivating, was a challenge. The more I read, the more discrepancies I found. Sources conflict over the original Newfoundland cable rights, and details differ about what transpired at Cyrus Field's first meeting with Frederic Gisborne. I chose to relate the most prevalent view, documented in several sources. Sometimes the research listed miles as nautical miles, sometimes simply as miles. Where I could document nautical miles, I used the term. Otherwise, I did not. Readers can assume that probably most mileages on water were intended to mean nautical miles, and on land, they are presumed to be statute miles. In addition, names of some places in my sources are spelled in a variety of ways, and dates differ from one source to another. Some names have changed since the mid-1800s. For example: *New Granada* is now *Colombia*; *Queenstown, Ireland*, is *Cobh*; *Aspinwall, Panama*, is *Colón*; and *Russian America* is now *Alaska*.

Uncovering details of Cyrus Field's adventure in South America with artist Frederic Church was a challenge. Cyrus's descendants told me that Cyrus was sick during most of that time and therefore didn't write much about it. The main source of information regarding that trip is Frederic Church's diary, partly written in Spanish and translated by experts at Olana State Historic Site, Hudson, New York. Frederic Church's letters home to his family, which I found at the Winterthur Museum, Garden, and Library in Winterthur, Delaware, also helped fill out details of their trip.

Coinage throughout the book is written as either British pounds or U.S. dollars, in actual monies mentioned at that time. One pound equaled about $5, and $1 in 1850 would be worth slightly more than $30 today. I leave it up to the reader to do the math.

Sources conflicted regarding dates and latitude and longitude measurements. But where an exact spot was located in the middle of the ocean isn't the point of my story. It seems miraculous that Cyrus Field's big dream came true. What I hope will attract readers is the adventure of this remarkable man and the feat he achieved by engaging teams of dedicated scientists and workers.

Much information has been written about the project in recent decades. But wherever possible, I went back to early sources. News of the transatlantic cable was of high interest in the 1850s and '60s. It was published in newspapers all over the United States, sometimes taking up an entire page of New York papers. I consulted dozens of those publications. Three books written by Cyrus Field's family members proved essential: One written by his daughter Isabella Field Judson detailed many letters written by and to Cyrus. It also included quotes from an unfinished autobiography that he shared with her. Cyrus's younger brother, Henry Field, wrote two books. I gained access to a short treatise that Cyrus Field wrote, copies of speeches that he gave throughout the country, and his diaries of the cable-laying expeditions. On each expedition, reporters went along, and those detailed accounts proved essential to my research.

It took thousands of people to lay the first transatlantic telegraph cable—company officials, scientists, sailors, technical crews, and others.

All were critical to its success, but I could not possibly name everyone involved.

More than 150 years ago, Cyrus Field and his colleagues in the cable venture believed the ability to communicate promptly between nations would help bring world peace. Probably nothing will make that possible. But sharing the story of the chief promoter of this amazing nineteenth-century achievement will, I hope, help readers understand an important, yet little-known, development in world communication and the perseverance needed to achieve it.

—MMC

TIMELINE

1819   **November 30**—Cyrus West Field is born in Stockbridge, Massachusetts, into a family of five brothers (David, age fourteen; Timothy, age ten; Matthew, age eight; Jonathan, age six; and Stephen, age three) and one sister, Emilia, age twelve.

1822   **April 3**—Younger brother, Henry Martyn Field, is born.

1823   **September 7**—Youngest sibling, Mary Elizabeth, is born.

1825   Erie Canal opens.

1830   Fire starts in the parsonage in Stockbridge, the Field family home.

1835   **April**—Moves to New York City and works as a clerk at a dry-goods store.
Fall—Brother Timothy sails from New Orleans, on a ship never heard from again.
December—Fire breaks out in New York's financial district. Cyrus helps keep looters away.

1837   Financial crash; seven out of ten businesses in New York fail temporarily.

1838   Returns to western Massachusetts to work in a paper mill in Lee.

1840   Buys an interest in a small paper mill at Westfield, Massachusetts, then accepts a position with E. Root & Company, a wholesale paper dealer in New York City.
December 2—Marries Mary Stone.

1841   **April**—E. Root & Company fails. Cyrus reorganizes the firm and names it Cyrus W. Field & Company.
October 10—Daughter Mary Grace is born.

1842   Samuel F. B. Morse places a wire across New York Harbor and sends electric current through it.

1843   **November 7**—Cyrus and Mary's second daughter, Alice, is born.

1844   **May**—Samuel Morse and associates string a telegraph line between Washington, D.C., and Baltimore, Maryland.

1846   **January 20**—Cyrus and Mary's third daughter, Isabella, is born.

1848   **November 20**—Fourth daughter, Fanny, is born.

1850 **January 24**—First son, Arthur, is born.

1851 **September**—Frederic Gisborne, engineer and telegraph operator, begins surveying Newfoundland's south coast in preparation for stringing a telegraph line.
A telegraph cable is laid across the English Channel.

1852 Gisborne fails to string a telegraph line across Newfoundland. By the next year, his company collapses, and he loses everything.
June 16—Cyrus's sister Mary Elizabeth marries brother of Cyrus's wife.

1853 Cyrus retires at age thirty-three.
April—With Frederic Church, leaves on a six-month trip to South America.
October 31—Parents' fiftieth wedding anniversary.

1854 **January**—Gisborne comes to New York looking for financial backing for his telegraph venture.
May 8—With other financiers, Cyrus charters the New York, Newfoundland and London Telegraph Company. The company begins construction of telegraph lines across Newfoundland.
May 17—Joseph Stone, Cyrus's brother-in-law and business partner, dies.
August 20—Cyrus and Mary's son, Arthur, dies suddenly at age four.
December—Cyrus sails to England to arrange for a submarine cable to connect Newfoundland to Nova Scotia across Cabot Strait.

1855 **July 4**—Second son, Edward, is born.
August—Attempt to lay a cable across Cabot Strait fails.
November 1—With other investors, Cyrus incorporates the American Telegraph Company to consolidate small landline companies on the east coast of the United States.

1856 Cable is laid across Cabot Strait, and the Newfoundland landline is completed.
Atlantic Telegraph Company is organized in London.

1857 **March 4**—President Franklin Pierce signs bill into law to supply U.S. ships for the cable-laying venture.
March 15—Cyrus and Mary's seventh child, Cyrus, is born.
August—Attempt to lay cable across the ocean fails.
A leading New York bank collapses, resulting in financial panic.

1858 **June**—Two cable ships, USS *Niagara* and HMS *Agamemnon*, embark on second cable-laying expedition and encounter a violent storm at sea; they return to Ireland; head out again in July.

August 5—*Niagara* arrives in Trinity Bay, Newfoundland, and *Agamemnon* in Ireland.

August 16—First message sent over the transatlantic cable. Queen Victoria sends greetings to President Buchanan, and he replies. The next night, fireworks set New York's City Hall on fire.

August 21—Cyrus is elected an honorary member of the New York Chamber of Commerce.

September 1—Cyrus receives a hero's welcome; a parade takes place in New York City.

September 2—A banquet is held at the Metropolitan Hotel. The cable fails during the event and breaks down completely a few weeks later.

1859 Cyrus receives Honorary Master of Arts degree from Williams College.

July—British Board of Trade forms a committee to investigate difficulties of underwater cables, leads to significant scientific and technological advances.

December 29—A fire in Cyrus's paper-company office and warehouse in New York City causes major losses.

1860 **December 20**—South Carolina secedes from the Union. Five more states secede in the next few weeks.

December 26—A small Union garrison moves to Fort Sumter.

1861 **March 4**—Abraham Lincoln becomes the sixteenth U.S. president.

April—Initial findings from the British Board of Trade's committee of inquiry are made public.

April 12—South Carolina troops open fire on Fort Sumter. Civil War begins.

August 16—Cyrus's mother, Submit Dickinson Field, dies.

October 24—The first transcontinental telegraph message is sent from San Francisco to President Lincoln by Cyrus's brother Stephen Field.

1862 **March**—London newspaper reports that Cyrus has been indicted in New York for treasonable proceedings; indictment is withdrawn, and the paper later apologizes.

September 17—Battle at Antietam.

September 22—Lincoln issues preliminary Emancipation Proclamation, which will free all slaves in Confederate territory on January 1, 1863.

1863 **January 1**—Lincoln issues the Emancipation Proclamation.

March 6—Lincoln appoints Cyrus's brother Stephen Field to the U.S. Supreme Court.

July—British Board of Trade's committee of inquiry report is published.

July 1—Battle of Gettysburg begins and lasts three days.

July 13—Draft riots begin in New York City, near Cyrus's home, which last for four days.

1864   Gutta Percha Company merges with Glass, Elliot & Company to become the Telegraph Construction and Maintenance Company.

Cyrus is offered the ship the SS *Great Eastern* to lay the transatlantic cable.

1865   **April 9**—General Lee surrenders; Civil War ends. Days later, Lincoln is assassinated. It takes twelve days for news to reach Great Britain.

July 15—*Great Eastern* leaves England for Valentia Island, Ireland, to lay cable.

July 23—Ship heads to Heart's Content, Newfoundland. The attempt fails after more than one thousand miles of cable has been laid.

1866   **March**—Anglo-American Telegraph Company is registered.

June 30—*Great Eastern* leaves England.

July 27—Ship reaches Heart's Content, Newfoundland. The next day, telegrams are exchanged between Queen Victoria and President Johnson.

August 9—*Great Eastern* goes back out to sea to grapple for the 1865 cable and finish laying it to Newfoundland. Success.

September 7—Ship arrives back in Heart's Content. Now there are two working underwater cables across the Atlantic Ocean. The 1866 cable is eighty times faster than the 1858 cable.

1867   Dominion of Canada is formed. Newfoundland remains a crown colony until 1949.

Cyrus is awarded a U.S. Congressional Gold Medal, the State of Wisconsin Medal, the Grand Medal of the French Exposition of 1867, and a gold medal by the Chamber of Commerce, Liverpool, England.

1874   Additional telegraph cables are laid between Ireland and Heart's Content, Newfoundland, over the next twenty years.

1875   Receives an honorary doctor of law degree from Williams College.

1876   Alexander Graham Bell invents the telephone, but no one can adapt it to underwater cables.

1877   Cyrus buys controlling interest in New York Elevated Railroad Company and is elected president of that company.

1883   The town of Field, British Columbia, and Mount Field in the Canadian Rockies are named in Cyrus's honor.

1887   Cyrus loses his fortune when the stock of New York Elevated Railroad Company plummets.

1890   **December 2**—Cyrus and Mary's golden wedding anniversary.

1891   **November 23**—Cyrus's wife, Mary, dies.

1892   **January 11**— Cyrus's oldest daughter, Mary Grace, dies.
May 17—Cyrus is elected an honorary member of the American Institute of Electrical Engineers (AIEE).
July 12—Cyrus dies at age seventy-two. He is buried in Stockbridge, Massachusetts.

CONNECTIONS TO MAKE*

BOOKS

Carter, Samuel, III. *Lightning Beneath the Sea: The Story of the Atlantic Cable*. New York: G. P. Putnam's Sons, 1969.
   Tells of the men who struggled to lay the underwater telegraph cable. Includes timeline.

Cookson, Gillian. *The Cable: The Wire That Changed the World*. Stroud, UK: Tempus, 2003.
   Relates how the first transatlantic cable was laid, from the failed attempts in the 1850s to the successful expedition in 1866. Includes a sixteen-page section of illustrations.

Dibner, Bern. *The Atlantic Cable*. 2nd. ed. New York: Blaisdell, 1964.
   Discusses the cable efforts during the 1857 and 1858 trips, the celebrations followed by failure, cable laying in 1865 and 1866, and final success. Includes some scientific information and has many illustrations.

Gordon, John Steele. *A Thread Across the Ocean: The Heroic Story of the Transatlantic Cable*. New York: Walker, 2002.
   Relates the extraordinary achievement, highlighting Cyrus Field's perseverance and courage, the failed attempts, the near disasters at sea, and the ways in which Field and his men overcame tremendous technological problems.

VIDEOS

"The First Atlantic Submarine Electric Telegraph Cable." Powerhouse Museum, Sydney, Australia. Posted April 5, 2009. youtube.com/watch?v=duI1m9WIOLs.
   In this five-minute video, the museum curator describes the remarkable events and shows leftover pieces of the original cable.

"The Great Transatlantic Cable." PBS Home Video. *American Experience*.
   Boston, WBGH Educational Foundation, 2005. Also available at youtube.com/watch?v=cFKONUBBHQw.
   This fifty-five-minute movie dramatizes the successful laying of the first transatlantic cable.

"Heart's Content, Newfoundland, Canada." Canada HD Travel Channel video. Posted June 14, 2012. youtube.com/watch?v=ZHMz99sRF9E.
   This video shows the cable station, examples of cables, a model of the *Great Eastern*, and Heart's Content harbor.

"How Undersea Cables Are Laid." TESubcom video. Posted May 3, 2010. youtube.com/
    watch?v=XQVzU_YQ3IQ.
    Watch a short animated video that shows a modern-day procedure for laying
    ocean cables.
"Mirror Galvanometers." Museum of the History of Science, Technology and Medicine,
    University of Leeds, United Kingdom video. Posted September 25, 2012. youtube.com/
    watch?v=eck9ngLpgBQ.
    Michael Kay, Ph.D. student at the University of Leeds, explains the mirror galvanom-
    eter, invented by William Thomson (Lord Kelvin), vital to successful underwater
    telegraphy.
"The Telegraph Field—Valentia Island." Posted April 11, 2012. youtube.com/
    watch?v=ywSJ7-Qri9w.
    This video includes an introduction to Valentia Island and comments from transat-
    lantic cable experts, and it shows the ruins of the original cable building.

WEBSITES

"History of the Atlantic Cable & Undersea Communications." Atlantic-cable.com.
    Navigate among multiple pages to view many aspects of the Atlantic cable story.
"Heart's Content Cable Station." From the Department of Tourism, Culture and Recreation,
    Government of Newfoundland and Labrador. jproc.ca/ve3fab/hearts_content.html.
    Read about the history of the cable and Newfoundland's part in it. Several pictures are
    included.
"How Cyrus Laid the Cable," poem by John Godfrey Saxe, published in *Harper's Weekly*,
    September 11, 1858. All Poetry. allpoetry.com/How-Cyrus-Laid-the-Cable.
    Read this amusing twelve-stanza poem about Cyrus Field's determination to lay the
    cable. For years, it was included in school reading books.
"SS Great Eastern." IKBrunel.org.uk. ikbrunel.org.uk/ss-great-eastern.
    A summary of the ship's details, including its use as a cable-laying vessel.
"Submarine Cable System History" by Bill Burns. SubmarineCableSystems.com. subma-
    rinecablesystems.com/default.asp.pg-history.
    Read about the trial and error of cables from the 1850s to the present.
"The Underwater Web: Cabling the Seas" by Bernard S. Finn, guest curator. A
    Smithsonian Institution Libraries Exhibition. sil.si.edu/Exhibitions/Underwater-web/.
    Explore numerous pages about underwater cables.

*Websites active at time of publication

ACKNOWLEDGMENTS

It is difficult to imagine a world without connections—one in which people cannot communicate with friends and family quickly and easily, no matter where they are. With cell phones and computers, the world is at our fingertips. Until the Atlantic cable was laid, North America was connected with the rest of the world only by ship.

Writing about a man who showed more perseverance and courage to connect two continents by wire communication than I can imagine took a bit of perseverance from me. I could never have connected all the "wires" to write the book without the willing assistance of many people. And, luckily for me, communication via the internet is possible. With the help of several reference librarians—primarily Christopher Schiff, Christina Bell, Peter Schlax, and Laura Juraska at Bates College and Barbara Kelley at Windham (ME) Public Library—I was able to connect to sources everywhere. Cindy Dykes at Portland (ME) Public Library and Chuck Prinn at the library of St. Joseph's College of Maine also provided assistance.

My local writer's group has been a continuing support, always ready with helpful critiques, and several friends from the Highlights Foundation writing retreats have offered assistance. A Colby College student, Lydia Larson, also helped with online research.

Hiking in Stockbridge, Massachusetts, I could visualize where young Cyrus roamed among the hills, along the river, and into the woods. Barbara Allen, curator of the Stockbridge Museum and Archives, hauled out materials for me to study. At Williams College, Amy Lovett, editorial director in the Office of Communications, and librarian Wayne Hammond at the Chapin Library provided valuable information about Cyrus and his brothers. I appreciate the assistance of Valerie Balint, interim director of collections and research at Olana State Historic Site in Hudson, New York, and Jeanne Solensky, librarian at Winterthur Museum, Garden and Library in Winterthur, Delaware, in locating information about Cyrus Field's trip to South America.

Dr. Bernard Finn, curator emeritus of the Electricity Collections at Smithsonian Institution's National Museum of American History, willingly answered questions and offered suggestions for my manuscript. Bill Burns, publisher and webmaster of Atlantic-Cable.com, was a great help, providing illustrations and general support. My sincere thanks go to Dr. Margaret Creighton, history professor at Bates College and noted author, who critiqued the manuscript.

I was fortunate to meet via e-mail a few of Cyrus Field's descendants, who have been helpful in this venture, particularly Stephanie Buffum Field and Diane Gravlee.

It took my entire family to completely connect all the "wires" of this book. My son, Timothy Cowan, a history buff, read and critiqued parts of the story and drew diagrams. My daughter-in-law, Marianne Cowan, read the entire manuscript, offering helpful suggestions. Three physicists— my husband, Carl, and my daughter and son-in-law, Catherine and David Brown—helped me try to understand the complicated physics involved in underwater telegraphy that even Cyrus couldn't understand. Many thanks to them—at least for trying. My brother and a few friends shared photographs for my research. The deepest thanks goes to my husband for many things: tackling all sorts of domestic duties without complaint and traveling with me to libraries and museums. And, of course, for starting this whole idea when he took me to visit Ireland and Newfoundland and Labrador.

Of course, an idea doesn't become a book without one more important connection: a fabulous editorial and publishing team. I have been fortunate to work with editor Carolyn P. Yoder again, whose expertise in nonfiction writing for children I greatly admire, and I sincerely appreciate the efforts of the entire team at Calkins Creek.

Thank you, everyone, for your support.

SOURCE NOTES*

Sources for all quotations in this book are found below. Each citation indicates the first words of the quotation and its document source. The document sources are listed either in the bibliography or below.

The following abbreviations are used:

CF Cyrus Field

Chamber Chamber of Commerce of New-York: *The Atlantic Telegraph: Report of the Proceedings at a Banquet Given to Mr. Cyrus W. Field . . .*

HF History Henry Field: *History of the Atlantic Telegraph*

HF Story Henry Field: *The Story of the Atlantic Telegraph*

Laying Cable Cyrus Field: "The Laying of the Atlantic Cable"

Olana Frederic Edwin Church: *Diary of 1853 Trip to South America*

Two Worlds Samuel Carter: *Cyrus Field: Man of Two Worlds*

Winterthur Letters of Frederic Edwin Church

CHAPTER ONE [page 8]

"Bold Cyrus Field he said, says he . . .": Saxe, "How Cyrus Laid the Cable," *Harper's Weekly*, September 11, 1858.

CHAPTER TWO [page 12]

"Cyrus was the 'squirmiest' . . .": *Two Worlds*, p. 25.
"At first we slept . . .": H. Field, quoted in same as above, p. 30.
"We are on the borders . . .": Rev. Field, quoted in Judson, p. 11.
"How many, many times . . .": H. Field, quoted in *Two Worlds*, p. 32.
"Father, here is your rat-trap!": CF, quoted in Judson, p. 10.
"Cyrus, I feel sure . . .": Rev. Field, quoted in same as above, p. 25.

CHAPTER THREE [page 20]

"I had to depend . . .": CF, quoted in Judson, p. 18.
"I always made it a point . . .": same as above.
"Bring Cyrus home . . .": Mrs. S. D. Field, quoted in same as above, p. 15.

*Websites active at time of publication

"I wish you would make . . .": CF letter, quoted in Judson, p. 21.

"an entrance to hell": Judson, p. 18.

"The business is in keeping . . .": Stewart, quoted in *Two Worlds*, p. 42.

"the largest that was . . .": CF letter, quoted in Judson, p. 19.

"I was up all night . . .": same as above.

"and my board . . .": same as above, p. 24.

CHAPTER FOUR [page 30]

"In 1844 . . .": CF, quoted in Judson, p. 32.

"On October 1st . . .": same as above, p. 27.

"I was not the principal . . .": same as above, p. 29.

"I was not worth a dollar . . .": same as above, p. 32.

"All business intrusted to me . . .": same as above.

"Jolly": same as above, p. 324.

"There was no luck . . .": same as above, p. 42.

CHAPTER FIVE [page 42]

"When he sought relaxation . . .": Judson, p. 295.

"had a shipmate . . .": same as above, p. 57.

"People in picturesque costumes . . .": Winterthur, Church, letter to sister Elizabeth, April 29, 1853, 57x18.30.

"The superintendents showed us . . .": same as above, Church, letter to father, June 9, 1853, 57x18.35.

"Soon after our departure . . .": same as above, Church, letter to mother, May 25, 1853, 57x18.34.

"arrived at a miserable hut": Olana, May 23, 1853, OL.1980.27.35.

"Yesterday Mr. Field . . .": same as above, June 8, 1853, OL.1980.27.41.

"Mr. Field is much sicker . . .": same as above, June 9, 1853, OL.1980.27.42.

"The guides were obliged . . .": Winterthur, Church, letter to sister Charlotte, August 8, 1853, 57x18.39.

"Left Quito . . ." and "Mr. Field is quite . . .": Olana, September 9, 1853, OL.1980.27.7.

"hired a small canoe . . .": same as above, September 23, 1853, OL.1980.27.13.

CHAPTER SIX [page 52]

"Once he had grasped the idea . . .": HF *History*, p. 26.

"I never saw Cyrus . . .": M. Field, quoted in *Two Worlds*, p. 94.

"It was while thus studying . . .": HF *History*, p. 26.

"may, with certainty . . .": Morse, quoted in Mabee, p. 321.

"Believing, as I did . . .": Cooper, quoted in Judson, p. 62.

"I shall never forget . . .": CF, quoted in HF *History*, p. 39.

"It seemed as if . . .": D. Field, quoted in same as above, p. 43.

"For months it was hardly . . .": HF *History*, p. 55.

"unwelcome intrusion": same as above.

"Who first conceived the idea . . .": CF, quoted in Judson, p. 134.

CHAPTER SEVEN [page 62]

"It was a very pretty plan . . .": CF, quoted in Chamber, p. 19.

"How many months? . . .": M. Field, quoted in *Two Worlds*, p. 111.

"You have no idea . . .": same as above.

"She was a swift . . .": HF *History*, p. 58.

"There were dogs . . .": *Harper's New Monthly Magazine*, p. 50.

"Has the bark arrived?": CF, quoted in Mullaly, p. 60.

"ran his steamer . . .": Cooper, quoted in Zachos, p. 9.

"I know how to steer . . .": unidentified ship's captain, quoted in same as above, p. 10.

"Your instructions were . . .": Cooper, quoted in Carter, *Lightning*, p. 38.

"became as stubborn . . .": Cooper, quoted in McDonald, p. 37.

"rolled with such violence . . .": Mullaly, p. 72.

"We not only lost our cable . . .": Cooper, quoted in Chamber, p. 45.

"Few had any faith . . .": CF, quoted in same as above, p. 19.

"It was a very pretty plan . . .": same as above.

"Every dollar . . .": same as above.

CHAPTER EIGHT [page 74]

"I am confident . . .": Morse, quoted in Mabee, p. 321.

"Charge it to profit and loss . . .": CF, quoted in HF *History*, p. 94.

"Here's the ship . . .": Brunel, quoted in Dugan, p. 73.

"My own hope is . . .": Seward, quoted in Dibner, p. 27.

"England tenders . . .": Douglas, quoted in Hearn, p. 59.

"Those few weeks . . ." and "entangled in such . . .": HF *Story*, p. 96.

"The Submarine Cable on board . . .": CF, quoted in "The Atlantic Telegraph Cable,"
    New-York Daily Tribune, August 12, 1857, p. 5.

"Ladies and gentlemen . . .": Judson, p. 81.

"What God has joined . . .": CF, quoted in "The Transatlantic Telegraph," *New York Herald*, Morning Edition, August 20, 1857, p. 1.

"dunderfunk": Mullaly, p. 85.

"old coffee-mill": same as above, p. 144.

"haunted us . . .": same as above, p. 143.

"Not a word was spoken . . .": same as above, p. 138.

"At 4 o'clock . . .": Bright, quoted in "Atlantic Telegraph," [London] *Times*, August 20, 1857, p. 10.

"At this time . . .": Mullaly, p. 147.

"All well on board . . .": "The Telegraph Cable," *Plattsburgh* [NY] *Republican*, August 29, 1857, p. 2.

"You could see . . .": Mullaly, p. 150.

"The cable's gone.": Bright, quoted in Gordon, p. 97.

"Losing no time . . .": Mullaly, p. 29.

"My confidence . . .": CF, quoted in HF *History*, pp. 160–61.

"Do not think . . .": same as above, p. 163.

"There are no signs . . .": "The Atlantic Telegraph and the Weather," *Evening Post* [NY], August 25, 1857, p. 3.

"Although the unfortunate . . .": CF, quoted in "The Atlantic Telegraph Expedition. The Cable Broken," *New York Herald*, Morning Edition, August 27, 1857, p. 1.

"We cannot see how . . .": Brooklyn *Eagle* writer, quoted in "The Atlantic Telegraph Accident," *Evening Post* [NY], August 31, 1857, p. 2.

CHAPTER NINE [page 94]

"While all hoped . . .": HF *History*, pp. 193–94.

"I assure . . ." and "that all the energy . . .": CF, quoted in Mullaly, p. 32.

"The strain on the man . . .": HF *Story*, p. 154.

"With the exception . . .": Mullaly, p. 209.

"no one expected . . .": telegram, quoted in "Additional Report of the Voyage of the Agamemnon," *New York Herald*, Morning Edition, August 21, 1858, p. 1.

"old coffee-mill": Mullaly, p. 144.

"I think there is nothing . . .": board chairman, quoted in Judson, p. 92.

"most of the directors . . .": CF, quoted in Bright, p. 115.

"There she is, sir . . .": unidentified sailor, quoted in Mullaly, p. 246.

"Thursday, July twenty-ninth . . .": CF journal, quoted in HF *History*, p. 193.

"We are hourly haunted . . .": Mullaly, p. 218.

"We hardly dare ask . . .": same as above, p. 259.

"The wire will be laid . . .": same as above, p. 247.

"We have all become . . .": Mullaly, p. 256.

"It was impossible . . .": same as above, p. 265.

"The *Niagara* getting light . . .": CF, quoted in Briggs and Maverick, p. 182.

"Passed several . . .": same as above, p. 184.

"The cable is laid!": CF, quoted in Gordon, p. 131.

"Arrived here yesterday . . .": CF, quoted in Judson, p. 95.

"Trinity Bay, August 7 . . .": CF, quoted in "The Fixed Fact of the Century," *New York Herald*, Sunday Morning, August 8, 1858, p. 1.

"After the end of the cable . . .": CF, quoted in Mullaly, p. 281.

"Dear Sir—The Atlantic telegraph . . .": CF, quoted in "The Atlantic Cable Laid!", *Boston Press and Post*, August 9, 1858, p. 1.

"a shock . . .": "The Ocean Telegraph," *New-York Daily Tribune*, August 19, 1858, p. 5.

CHAPTER TEN [page 110]

"This news will send . . .": "The Atlantic Cable Laid," *New York Herald*, Morning Edition, August 6, 1858, p. 1.

"Bravo, Atlantic Cable! . . .": "The News in St. John," *New-York Times*, August 6, 1858, p. 1.

"bonfires are blazing . . .": "The Fixed Fact of the Century," *New York Herald*, Sunday Morning, August 8, 1858, p. 1.

"bells rang for half an hour . . .": "The Cable Celebration," *Eastern Argus* [Portland, ME], September 2, 1858.

"Standing in the office . . .": H. W. Longfellow, quoted in Longfellow, p. 323.

"The great news of the hour . . .": same as above, p. 325.

"Every man on board . . .": CF, quoted in "Latest by Telegraph," *New-York Times*, August 6, 1858, p. 1.

"The Great Event . . .": "The Atlantic Cable Laid," *New York Herald*, Morning Edition, August 6, 1858, p. 1.

"the great triumph . . .": "The Atlantic Cable—The Great Triumph of the Age—The United States and Great Britain," *Boston Press and Post*, August 9, 1858, p. 1.

"The cable is laid; and now . . .": "Success or Failure—A Contrast," *New York Herald*, Morning Edition, August 9, 1858, p. 4.

"As your pastor . . .": Adams, quoted in Judson, p. 99.

"The news of the successful . . .": "The News in Rutland," *New-York Times*, August 6, 1858, p. 1.

"It was at first believed . . .": "The News in Philadelphia," same as above.

"The people here seem . . .": CF, quoted in "The Ocean Cable," *New York Herald*, Morning Edition, August 9, 1858, p. 1.

"consistent and liberal . . .": CF, quoted in Briggs and Maverick, p. 191.

"Your family is all at Stockbridge...": D. Field, quoted in Mullaly, p. 284.

"The cause of our not...": de Sauty, quoted in "The Atlantic Telegraph," *Eastern Argus* [Portland, ME], August 16, 1858.

"Europe and America are united...": "The Ocean Telegraph," *New-York Times*, August 17, 1858, p. 1.

"The Queen desires...": Queen Victoria, quoted in "The Ocean Telegraph," *New-York Times*, August 18, 1858, p. 1.

"Wait repairs...": Valentia operator, quoted in *Two Worlds*, p. 168.

"The Queen is convinced...": Queen Victoria, quoted in "The Ocean Telegraph," *New-York Times*, August 18, 1858, p. 1.

"May the Atlantic Telegraph...": Buchanan, quoted in same as above.

"At your unanimous...": CF, quoted in HF *History*, pp. 231–32.

"as if they...": "Arrival of the Frigate Niagara," *New-York Times*, August 19, 1858, p. 1.

"In twenty-four hours...": HF *History*, p. 221.

"Success, at last...": "Cable Gossip," *New-York Times*, September 1, 1858, p. 1.

"The Great Event..." and "Honor to..." and "Europe from these...": "Ocean Cable Celebration," *New-York Times*, September 2, 1858, p. 1.

"anxiety and toil": D. Field, quoted in same as above, p. 8.

"the far-seeing and electrifying...": Cooper, quoted in same as above, p. 5.

"The directors are...": telegram from Valentia, quoted in Judson, p. 121.

"God has been with us...": "Ocean Cable Celebration," *New-York Times*, September 2, 1858, p. 8.

"This is a celebration...": Henry, quoted in Dibner, p. 69.

CHAPTER ELEVEN [page 126]

"The cable was laid...": Laying Cable, p. 177.

"Owing to some cause..." through "Under these circumstances...": company secretary, quoted in [London] *Times*, September 6, 1858, p. 7.

"Repeat, please" through "Please send something": Clarke, pp. 61–62.

"Please give explicit...": CF, quoted in "The Atlantic Cable," *Boston Press and Post*, September 27, 1858, p. 1.

"TRINITY BAY, Sept. 24...": de Sauty, quoted in "A Card," *Boston Semi-Weekly Courier*, September 27, 1858, p. 1.

"It is all a humbug!...": unidentified man, quoted in Zachos, p. 11.

"We received over it...": Cooper, quoted in same as above.

"We had been set down...": same as above.

"frantic fooleries...": Whitehouse, quoted in Lindley, pp. 133–34.

"After the failure of 1858 . . .": Laying Cable, p. 177.

"the whole thing . . ." and "the great success . . .": "The Atlantic Telegraph," *New-York Times*, August 10, 1865, p. 2.

"There was a profound . . .": CF, quoted in Chamber, p. 23.

"where our business . . .": *New-York Commercial Advertiser*, December 30, 1859, p. 3.

"The Wonder of the Seas": Dugan, p. 2.

"placed a mortgage . . .": Judson, p. 130.

CHAPTER TWELVE [page 136]

"I never worked . . .": CF, quoted in Judson, p. 157.

"Uncle Judge": Carpenter, p. 22.

"Oh, if that old cable . . .": Field family children, quoted in Judson, p. 216.

"That is just . . .": CF, quoted in same as above.

"We had one big war . . .": Lincoln, quoted in Sandburg, p. 365.

"Now is the time . . .": CF, quoted in Judson, p. 136.

"The importance of the early . . .": same as above, p. 137.

"treasonable proceedings . . .": indictment, quoted in same as above, p. 141.

"I regret exceedingly . . .": CF, quoted in same as above, p. 143.

"It was inspiring . . .": HF *Story*, p. 239.

"they applauded . . .": same as above, p. 238.

"I did not get . . .": Laying Cable, p. 178.

"I have been very anxious . . ." and "Be very kind . . .": CF, quoted in Judson, pp. 152–53.

"The whole country . . .": same as above, p. 154.

"Some days I have worked . . .": same as above.

"Mr. Field has crossed . . .": company secretary, quoted in same as above, p. 140.

"may reasonably be . . .": report, quoted in HF *History*, p. 266.

"As the rioters . . .": Mrs. D. Field, quoted in Judson, p. 159.

"The Atlantic telegraph cable is certainly . . .": "The Atlantic Telegraph," *New-York Times*, November 11, 1863, p. 1.

"The Atlantic telegraph project . . .": *The Telegraphic Journal*, vol. 1, February 6, 1864, p. 64.

"I went to see him . . .": CF, quoted in Chamber, p. 24.

"a pledge . . .": Laying Cable, p. 179.

"Wonder of the Seas": Dugan, p. 2.

"In all my business . . .": CF, quoted in Gordon, p. 170.

CHAPTER THIRTEEN [page 150]

"For a week . . .": Laying Cable, p. 180.

"Just before leaving . . .": CF, quoted in Judson, p. 186.

"I WISH SUCCESS . . .": Prince Albert, quoted in Russell, p. 47.

"We have now . . .": CF, letter to Henry Field, May 17, 1865. atlantic-cable.com/
   Cables/1865Atlantic/index.htm.

"greatest undertaking . . .": FitzGerald, quoted in Russell, p. 53.

"huge paddles began . . .": Deane, "Narrative . . . ," p. 442.

"puffed and wheezed . . .": HF *History*, p. 319.

"We expect to reach . . .": CF, quoted in "The Cable," *Philadelphia Inquirer*, August 7,
   1865, p. 1.

"*Copper and zinc!* . . .": Smith, p. 340.

"Pass the cable . . .": Canning, quoted in Deane, "Narrative . . . ," p. 443.

"No man who saw it . . .": Russell, p. 76.

"No useless sentry . . .": Smith, p. 352.

"Stop it!" and "Look out!": crew, quoted in Russell, p. 96.

"It's all over . . .": Canning, quoted in "News from the Atlantic Cable," *Boston Press and
   Post*, August 21, 1865, p. 1.

"The Cable has parted and . . .": CF, quoted in same as above.

"No words could describe . . .": Russell, p. 81.

"We have caught it! . . .": sailors, quoted in same as above, p. 83.

"*Great Eastern* left mouth . . .": CF, quoted in Judson, p. 195.

"Farewell": the *Terrible*'s signal, quoted in same as above.

"Good-bye . . .": the *Great Eastern*'s signal, quoted in same as above.

"There was a profound . . .": Russell, p. 97.

"We thought . . .": unidentified reporter, quoted in Dugan, p. 185.

"THE CABLE LOST": *New-York Times*, August 16, 1865, p. 1.

"The failure of the great . . .": same as above, p. 4.

"We've learned a great deal . . .": CF, quoted in Gordon, p. 189.

CHAPTER FOURTEEN [page 168]

"It has been . . .": CF, quoted in Chamber, p. 31.

"I am sorry . . .": Anderson, quoted in *Two Worlds*, p. 242.

"This was a terrible . . .": Laying Cable, p. 180.

"in fourteen days . . .": CF, quoted in Judson, p. 199.

"The cable-watch are clothed . . .": Deane, "Diary . . . ," Saturday, July 14, 1866.

"Everything was perfectly . . .": Laying Cable, p. 181.

"Ship will reverse . . .": Smith, p. 156.

"Once a day ship will send . . .": same as above, p. 160.

"We had fogs and storms . . .": Laying Cable, p. 181.

"If you land the cable . . .": Glass, quoted in Judson, p. 206.

"Here we are now . . .": Deane, "Diary . . . ," Friday, July 27, 1866.

"We sent the end . . .": CF, quoted in Judson, p. 206.

"There was the wildest . . .": Gooch, quoted in *Two Worlds*, p. 250.

"Is there a steamer . . .": CF, quoted in HF *Story*, p. 343.

"The Bloodhound . . .": Reply to CF, quoted in same as above.

"Telegraph instantly . . .": CF, quoted in same as above.

"Heart's Content, July 27 . . .": HF *History*, p. 361.

"to the President . . .": Queen Victoria's message, Smith, p. 370.

"Still we worked . . .": Laying Cable, p. 182.

"It was only when . . .": same as above, p. 183.

"Canning to Glass . . .": telegram, quoted in Dibner, p. 144.

"Understand, Query.": telegram, quoted in Smith, p. 187.

"The roaring bravos . . .": R. Dudley, quoted in HF *Story*, p. 367.

"The cable of 1865 . . .": CF, telegram to Mrs. Cyrus W. Field, quoted in Judson, p. 213.

"Both O. K.": CF, quoted in same as above.

"Never shall I forget . . .": same as above, pp. 213–14.

"The Atlantic cable of last year . . .": "The Old Atlantic Cable Picked Up," *Daily Eastern Argus* [Portland, ME], September 3, 1866, p. 2.

"This was like a whisper . . .": Laying Cable, p. 183.

"They dragged the shore end . . .": same as above, p. 184.

"It has been . . .": CF, quoted in Chamber, pp. 31–32.

"Thank God . . .": HF *History*, p. 361.

EPILOGUE [page 185]

"the wonder . . .": Cooper, quoted in McDonald, p. 165.

"Lord Cable.": Hearn, p. 241.

"CYRUS WEST FIELD . . .": gravestone, Stockbridge Cemetery, Stockbridge, Massachusetts.

"To have been the pioneer . . .": Anderson, quoted in Judson, p. 74.

SELECTED BIBLIOGRAPHY *

Alef, Daniel. *Cyrus Field: Transatlantic Visionary.* Santa Barbara, CA: Titans of Fortune Publishing, 2008.

Briggs, Charles F., and Augustus Maverick. *The Story of the Telegraph, and a History of the Great Atlantic Cable; A Complete Record of the Inception, Progress, and Final Success of That Undertaking. A General History of Land and Oceanic Telegraphs. Descriptions of Telegraphic Apparatus, and Biographical Sketches of the Principal Persons Connected with the Great Work.* New York: Rudd and Carleton, 1858.

Bright, Charles. *The Story of the Atlantic Cable.* New York: D. Appleton, 1903. gutenberg.org/files/46105/46105-h/46105-h.htm.

Burns, Bill. "History of the Atlantic Cable and Undersea Communications from the First Submarine Cable of 1850 to the Worldwide Fiber Optic Network." Atlantic Cable. 2017. atlantic-cable.com.

Burrows, Edwin G., and Mike Wallace. *Gotham: A History of New York City to 1898.* New York: Oxford University Press, 1999.

Carpenter, Russell F. "The Brothers Field." *Williams Alumni Review* [Williams College], March 2006.

Carter, Samuel, III. *Cyrus Field: Man of Two Worlds.* New York: G. P. Putnam's Sons, 1968.

———. *Lightning Beneath the Sea: The Story of the Atlantic Cable.* New York: G. P. Putnam's Sons, 1969.

Chamber of Commerce of New-York. *The Atlantic Telegraph. Report of the Proceedings at a Banquet Given to Mr. Cyrus W. Field, by the Chamber of Commerce of New-York, at the Metropolitan Hotel, November 15th, 1866.* New York: J. W. Amerman, 1866.

Church, Frederic Edwin. Diary of 1853 Trip to South America. May–October 1853. Translated from the Spanish. Olana Research Collection, OL.1980.27. Olana State Historic Site, Hudson, NY. New York State Office of Parks, Recreation and Historic Preservation.

———. Letters. Courtesy of the Winterthur Library, Joseph Downs Collection of Manuscripts and Printed Ephemera, Collection 66.

Clarke, Arthur C. *Voice Across the Sea.* Rev. ed. New York: Harper and Row, 1974. First published 1959.

Deane, John C. "Diary of the Atlantic Telegraph Expedition, 1866." Atlantic Cable, 2016. atlantic-cable.com/Article/1866Deane/index.htm.

———. "Narrative of the Atlantic Telegraph Expedition, 1865." *Macmillan's Magazine,* Volume 12, September, 1865.

*Websites active at time of publication

Dibner, Bern. *The Atlantic Cable*. New York: Blaisdell, 1964.

Dugan, James. *The Great Iron Ship*. New York: Harper and Brothers, 1953.

Field, Cyrus W. "The Laying of the Atlantic Cable." In *The Great Events by Famous Historians*, edited by Rossiter Johnson, vol. 18, pp. 175–185. New York: National Alumni, 1905. archive.org/details/greateventsbyfam18horniala.

Field, Henry M. *History of the Atlantic Telegraph*. New York: Charles Scribner, 1866.

———. *The Story of the Atlantic Telegraph*. New York: Charles Scribner's Sons, 1893.

Gordon, John Steele. *A Thread Across the Ocean: The Heroic Story of the Transatlantic Cable*. New York: Walker, 2002.

Harper's New Monthly Magazine, Vol. XII. December 1855 to May 1856. "A Trip to Newfoundland." Harper & Brothers, Publishers, 1856, pages 45-57.

Hearn, Chester G. *Circuits in the Sea: The Men, the Ships, and the Atlantic Cable*. Westport, CT: Praeger, 2004.

Hillstrom, Kevin, and Laurie Collier Hillstrom. *American Civil War Almanac*. Detroit: UXL, 2000.

Howat, John K. *Frederic Church*. New Haven, CT: Yale University Press, 2005.

Judson, Isabella Field, ed. *Cyrus W. Field: His Life and Work*. New York: Harper and Brothers, 1896.

Lindley, David. *Degrees Kelvin: A Tale of Genius, Invention, and Tragedy*. Washington, DC: Joseph Henry Press, 2004.

Longfellow, Samuel, ed. *Life of Henry Wadsworth Longfellow: With Extracts from His Journals and Correspondence*. Boston: Ticknor, 1886. 2nd Edition, University Press, John Wilson and Son, Cambridge.

Mabee, Carleton. *The American Leonardo: A Life of Samuel F. B. Morse*. New York: Octagon Books, 1969.

McDonald, Philip B. *A Saga of the Seas: The Story of Cyrus W. Field and the Laying of the First Atlantic Cable*. New York: Wilson-Erickson, 1937.

Mullaly, John. *The Laying of the Cable, or The Ocean Telegraph; Being a Complete and Authentic Narrative of the Attempt to Lay the Cable Across the Entrance to the Gulf of St. Lawrence in 1855, and of the Three Atlantic Telegraph Expeditions of 1857 and 1858*. New York: D. Appleton, 1858.

Oslin, George P. *The Story of Telecommunications*. Macon, GA: Mercer University Press, 1992.

Phalen, William J. *How the Telegraph Changed the World*. Jefferson, NC: McFarland, 2014.

Rowe, Ted. *Connecting the Continents: Heart's Content and the Atlantic Cable*. St. John's, NL: Creative Publishers, 2009.

Russell, William H. *The Atlantic Telegraph*. Stroud, Gloucestershire, UK: Nonsuch Publishing, 2005. First published 1866.

Sandburg, Carl. *Abraham Lincoln: The War Years*. Vol. 1. New York: Harcourt, Brace, 1939.

Shaffner, Tal. *Shaffner's Telegraph Companion: Devoted to the Science and Art of the Morse American Telegraph*. Vol. 2. New York: Pudney and Russell, 1855.

Silverman, Kenneth. *Lightning Man: The Accursed Life of Samuel F. B. Morse*. New York: Alfred A. Knopf, 2003.

Smith, Willoughby. *The Rise and Extension of Submarine Telegraphy*. London: J. S. Virtue, 1891.

Standage, Tom. *The Victorian Internet: The Remarkable Story of the Telegraph and the Nineteenth Century's On-line Pioneers*. New York: Walker, 2007. First published 1998.

Valente, AJ. *Rag Paper Manufacture in the United States, 1801–1900: A History, with Directories of Mills and Owners*. Jefferson, NC: McFarland, 2010.

Zachos, J. C., ed. *The Political and Financial Opinions of Peter Cooper, with an Autobiography of His Early Life*. New York: Trow's Printing and Bookbinding, 1877.

NEWSPAPERS AND PERIODICALS

American Heritage Magazine

The Berkshire Eagle [Pittsfield, MA]

The Berkshire Evening Eagle [Pittsfield, MA]

Boston Press and Post

Boston Semi-Weekly Courier

Chicago Daily Tribune

Cleveland [OH] *Daily Plain Dealer*

Daily Confederation [Montgomery, AL]

Daily Eastern Argus [Portland, ME]

Daily News [Tarrytown, NY]

Eastern Argus [Portland, ME]

Evening Post [New York, NY]

Harper's New Monthly Magazine

Harper's Weekly

The Illustrated London News

Jeffersonian [Portland, ME]

Macmillan's Magazine [London and Cambridge, England]

Massachusetts Spy [Worcester, MA]

Newfoundlander [St. John's NL]

New-York Commercial Advertiser

New-York Daily Times

New-York Daily Tribune

New York Herald

New-York Saturday Press
New-York Times
Norwich [CT] *Aurora*
Paper Maker [Wilmington, DE]
Philadelphia Inquirer
Plattsburgh [NY] *Republican*
Sacramento Daily Union
Scientific American
Springfield [MA] *Republican*
Sun [Baltimore, MD]
The Telegraphic Journal: A Weekly Record of Electrical Progress [London, England]
Times [London, England]

INDEX

Page numbers in **boldface** refer to images and/or captions

A

Adams, Charles, 142

Adams, William, Dr., 112

Agamemnon, 82, 83, 84, **84**, 85, **85**, **88**, 90, 97–100, **100**, 101, **101**, 102–105, **105**, 106, 107, 108, **118**, 122, 127

Alaska, 186

Albany, 172, 177

Albany, New York, 22

Albert Edward, Prince of Wales, 155

American flag, 115, 172, 175

American Telegraph Company, 72, 139

Americans, 81, **128**, 130

Anderson, James, 151, 156, 159, 160, 165, 169, 170, 172–173, 177, 178, 187

Andes Mountains, 41, 43, 45, 46, 48

Anglo-American Telegraph Company, 170, 171

Antietam, 143, **144**

Asia, 22

Aspinwall, Panama, 50

Associated Press, Liverpool, 84

Associated Press, United States, 108, 112, 175

Astor House hotel, 9, 53, **54**

"Atlantic Cable Bouquet," 119

Atlantic coast, 9, 145

Atlantic Ocean, 8, 37, 56, 59, 61, 72, 77, 78, 91, 104, 108, **113**, 119, 131, 145, 148, **148**, 162, 165, **174**, 181, **182**

Atlantic Telegraph, 162, 163, **163**

Atlantic Telegraph Company, 76, 79, 81, 90, 112, 117, 122, 127, 130, 132, 135, 142, 144, 145, 148, 151, 167, 169

directors, 76, 82–83, 90, 91, 95, 99, 103, 117, 122, 129, 132, 144, 145, 167, 169

Atlantic telegraph fleet, 90, 104, 112

"Atlantic Telegraph Polka," **118**

A. T. Stewart & Company, 22, 28, 29

B

Baltimore, 33, 57

Barranquilla, 44, 45

Battery, 117, 122

Battery Park, **36**

Bay of Biscay, 98

Bering Strait, 147

Berkshires, 17, 31, 38, 48

Bible, 15, 19, 27, 145

Bloodhound, 175

Board of Trade, 132, 133, 137, 145, 147, 187

Bogotá, 45, 47

Bogotá River, 48

Boston, 31, 33, 111, 141, 143

Brady, Mathew, **124**

Brassey, Thomas, 147, 170

Brett, John, 60, 72, 75, 76

Brewer, Marshall, 65

Bright, Charles, 75, 76, 77, 84, 85, 86, 88, 89, 91, 98, 102

British, 11, 75, 78, 79, 81, **84**, 95, 107, 141, **141**, 142, 143, **144**, 147, 151, 155, 185

Admiralty, 129; First Lord of, 98

flag, 115, 175

government, 76, 96, 129, 132, 141, 142, 145

navy, 79

support, 147, 151, 153, 172

troops, 129, 138.

See also Board of Trade; *Trent*

British Columbia, 146

Broadway, 22, 37, 53, 116, 120, **121**, 123, 138

Brooklyn Navy Yard, 26, **80**, 97, 117

Brunel, Isambard, 77, 134

Buchanan, James, 108, 112, 114, 115, 118, 119, 125, 129

Buffalo, New York, 111, 145

Bull's Arm, Newfoundland, 90, 106, 107, **109**, 156

Burling Slip, 35

C

cable celebrations in 1858, 111–125, **116**, **118**

banquet, 125

Crystal Palace event, 120, 122–123 **122**, **123**

parades, 120, **121**, 123, **123**

cable design, 60, 77, 78, **78**, 81, 82, 96, 97, 145, 147, 153–154, **157**, 171. *See also* shore-end cable

cable paying-out machinery, 83, **85**, 87, 91, 96, 103, 107, 152, **152**, 153, 160

Cabot Strait, 55, 59, 60, 61, **61**, 69–72, **70**, 75, 79, 81, 84, 156, 175, 181

California, 49, 91

chief justice of, 140.

See also San Francisco

Canada, 9, 53, 59, 111, 118, 120, 129, 138, 142, 185

governor general of, 118.

See also British Columbia; Cabot Strait; Labrador; New Brunswick; Newfoundland; Newfoundland and Labrador; Nova Scotia

Canning, Samuel, 60, 64, 67–71, 84, 156, 158, 159, 162, 163, 164, 165, 170, 171, 176–179, **179**, 180

Cape Breton Island, Nova Scotia, 68, 72

Cape Hatteras, North Carolina, 91

Cape May, New Jersey, 135

Cape Ray, Newfoundland, 55, 67, 68, 69, **69**, 72

Cape Sable Island, Nova Scotia, 66

Caribbean coast, 45, 50

Caribbean Sea, 106

Caroline, 157

Carter, Samuel, III, 12

Castle Garden, 120

Central Park, 115, 138

Chamber of Commerce, 130, 183, 185

Charleston Harbor, 135

Chesapeake Bay, 139

Chile, **44**, 45, 49

China, 129

Church, Frederic, 31, 39, 43, 45–50, **46**, **49**, **50**, 53

City Hall, 22, 25, **116**, 116–117, 119, 123, **128**

City Hall Park, **35**, 115, 116, 123

Civil War, 138–146, **139**, **140**, **141**, **144**, 155. *See also* Antietam; draft riot; Gettysburg; Revenue Act; *San Jacinto*

Coney Island, 36

Confederacy, 137, 138, 142, 143; army, 138, 143

Connecticut, 17, 28, 31, 38. *See also* Guilford; Hartford; New Haven

Cooper, Peter, 57, 58, **58**, 59, 65, 68, 70, 71, 72, 77, 79, 81, 122, 130, 139, 151, 185

Cooper Union, 57, 133

Cotopaxi, Ecuador, 49, **49**

Croton Aqueduct/Reservoir, **35**, 36

Croton River, 33

Crystal Palace, London, 39, **40**

Crystal Palace, New York City, 39, **40**, 120, **122**, **123,** 131

Cuba, 141

Cunard Lines, 130, 151

Cyclops, 82

Cyrus Telegraph Station, **109**

"Cyrus the Great," 111, 112

Cyrus W. Field & Company, 33, **34**, 35, 36, 37, 39, 41, 53, 60, 91, 92, 133, 135, 137, 138

D

Deane, John, 171, 174

de Sauty, C. V., 113, 114, 128, 129, 156

donkey engine, 152, 160, 162, 170

Douglas, Stephen, 80

Dover, England, 157

draft riot, 145, **146**

Dudley, Robert, 171, 180

"dunderfunk," 87

dynamometer, **85**, 98, 152, 178

E

Eagle, 91

East Coast, 31, 33, 39, 72, 140

East River, 25, 26, 117

East Twenty-First Street, 38

Eclectic Fraternity, 27

Ecuador, 48, 49, **49**. *See also* Quito; Cotopaxi; Guayaquil

Emancipation Proclamation, 144

England, 11, 38, 55, 59, 60, **61**, 64, 66, 67, 71, 75, 76, 80, **80**, 81, 82, 90, 95, 96, 115, 130, 143, 145, 147, 152, 155, 166, 169, 176, 185. *See also* Dover; Greenwich; Liverpool; London; Plymouth; Sheerness; Thames River

English Channel, 55, 60, 72, 98, 156, 157, 172

equator, 49

Erie Canal, 14, 22, 26, 35, 120

E. Root & Company, 32–33, 40; bankruptcy, 33

Europe, 10, 11, 22, 37, 38, 39, 55, 56, 57, 72, 90, 114, **118**, 120, 132, 146, 167, 170, 184

Evening Post, 90

Everett, William, 84, 95, 96, 97

Exhibition of the Industry of All Nations, **40**

Expeditions

1855 Cabot Strait cable-laying trip, 65–71, **69**, **70**

1856 Cabot Strait cable-laying trip, 71

1857 cable expedition, 75–91, **86**, **88**

cable lost, 89

1858 cable expeditions, 95–109

cable arrived in Newfoundland, 108, **109**

first failure, 103

storm, 99–101, **100**, **101**. *See also under* Field, Cyrus West: 1858 expeditions

1865 cable expedition, 151–167, **154**, **156**, **160**, **161**

cable lost, 164–166, **166**

sabotage suspected, 162–164, **163**

1866 cable expedition, 169–184, **174**, **178**

1865 cable recovered, 176–182, **179**, **180**, **181**, **182**

final success, 183, **183**

first cable success, 174–176

F

Faraday, Michael, 76–77

Faroe Islands, 130

Field, Alice, 36, 65, 143, 187

Field, Arthur, 38; death of, 60

Field, Cyrus West, 6, **6**, 8, **10**, 12, **14**, **15**, **16**, 20, **22**, **24**, **27**, **28**, 30, **32**, **34**, **38**, **44**, **46**, **50**, **51**, **54**, **58**, **61**, 62, **122**, **123**, **124**, 126, **134**, 136, **146**, **148**, 150, **163**, 168, **181**, **182**, **186**

1835 fire, helped in, 26, **27**

1853 South America trip, 43–51

arrested, 48.

See also Church, Frederic; South America

1858 expeditions

persuasiveness, 103

received shock from electric current, 108

American Telegraph Company formed, 72

Atlantic Telegraph Company formed, 75–76

built home near Gramercy Park, 38–39

business partner died. *See* Stone, Joseph, death of

career

company office and warehouse fire, 133

first job in New York City, A. T. Stewart & Company, 22–25, 27–29

formed Cyrus W. Field & Company, 33

junior partner in paper merchandising firm, E. Root & Company, New York City, 32–33

paper merchant, 34, 35–36, **38**, 39–40, 60;

worked in paper mills in Massachusetts, **28**, 31.

See also Cyrus W. Field & Company

childhood and youth, 13–19, **14**

home burned, 17–18, **18**

conceived idea to lay a transatlantic telegraph cable, 11, 56–57

death, 187

death of wife. *See* Field, Mary Bryan Stone

education

bookkeeping course, 29

school, **15**, 18–19

Europe, first trip to, 37–38

golden wedding anniversary, 187

Great Eastern, excursion on, 134–135, **134**

junk dealer, **34**, 35, 131

marriage, **32**, 33. *See also* Field, Mary Bryan Stone

meeting with Frederic Gisborne, 9–11, 55–56, 59

met with members of U.S. Congress, 79–80

New York, Newfoundland and London Telegraph Company formed, 57–59, **58**

New York City elevated railways, involvement in, 187

paid creditors former debts from bankrupt company, 40

received *Great Eastern* to lay cable, 147–148, **148**

relationship with family, 13–19, 23, **24**, 28, 29, 43, 45, 49, **51**, 60, 78, 117, 120, 132–133, 134, **134**, 139, 142–143, 145, 165, 175, 184

    children, 36, 37, 38, 45, 47, 49, 60, 65, 76, 132, 140, 143, 145, 169, 187. *See also* Field (individual children by name)

    siblings, 13, **14**, 14–19, 26, 33, 44, 49, **51**, 76, 114. *See also* Field (individual siblings by name)

    wife. *See* Field, Mary Bryan Stone

ridiculed, 131

seasick, 37, 45, 59, 66, 99, 107, 144, 162

treason, indicted for, 142

U.S. Congressional Gold Medal awarded, 185

work habits, 35–37

Field, Cyrus William, 81, 138, 143

    death of, 187

Field, David Dudley (brother), 13, 15, 19, 21, 22, 23, 24, 26, 29, 33, 39, **51**, 57, **58**, 59, 79, 114, 122, 133, 137, 145, **182**

Field, David Dudley, Reverend, 13, 14–19, **15**, 21, 23, 24, 25, 28, 29, 33, 44, 45, 65, 114, 123, 135

Field, Edward Morse, 65, 138, 143, 187

Field, Emilia, 13, 15, 65

Field, Fanny, 36, 65, 143, 187

Field, Heman, 138

Field, Henry (brother), 14–17, 19, 23, 33, **51**, 52, 56, 60, 65, 80, 94, 99, 118, 143, 155, **182**

Field, Henry (nephew), 138

Field, Isabella, 36, 65, 143, 169. *See also* Judson, Isabella Field

Field, Jonathan, 13, 15, 19, 21, 23, **24**, 26, 33, **51**

Field, Mary Bryan Stone, 17, 31, **32**, 33, 36, 37, 38, 39, 45, 49, 60, 65, 72, 75, 76, 78, 81, 108, 112, 132, 140, 143, 145, 165, 166, 169, 175, 180, **182**, 183

    death of, 187

    golden wedding anniversary, 187

    marriage, **32**, 33

Field, Mary Elizabeth, 14, 19, 23. *See also* Stone, Mary Elizabeth Field

Field, Mary Grace, 33, 65, 143

    death of, 187

Field, Matthew, 9, **10**, 13, 15, **28**, 29, 31, 32, 33, **51**, 53–56, **54**, 59, 63, 64, 67, 72, 138

Field, Mrs. David, 145

Field, Stephen, 13, 19, 29, 33, 49, **51**, 140. *See also* "Uncle Judge"

Field, Submit Dickinson, 13, 14, 16, **16**, 17, 19, 23, 24, **24**, 45, 51, 114, 135

    death of, 139

Field, Timothy, 13, 15, 19, 23, 29, 43, 44, 45, 49, 51

Fifth Avenue, 120

Financial Panic of 1837, 28, 33

Financial Panic of 1857, 91, 131, 133

Financial Panic of 1860, 135

fire of 1835, New York City, 25–26, **27**. *See also under* Field, Cyrus West: 1835 fire

FitzGerald, Peter, Sir, 157

Florida, 72

Foilhummerum Bay, 157, 172, **173**

Fort Powhatan, 139

Fort Sumter, 135, 138

Forty-Second Street, 120

France, 55, 98. *See also* Paris; Rhine River

Fredricks, Charles DeForest, **186**

G

Gettysburg, 145

ghost, 152, 161, 164, 172

Gisborne, Frederic, 9–11, **10**, 53–56, **54**, 59, 63, 65, 72, 131, 184

Glass, Elliot & Company, 60, 148

Glass, Richard, 174, 180

"God Save the Queen," 117

Gooch, Daniel, 147, 170, 171, 175

Gorgon, 106

Gramercy Park, **10**, 39, **146**

Great Britain, 13, 72, 75, 76, 79, 82, 98, 112, 114, 115, 120, 129, 130, 132, 138, 141, **141**, 142, 143, 147, 151, 175, 187

    Astronomer Royal, 77

    Lords Commissioners of Her Majesty's Treasury, 76.

    See also British; England

Great Eastern, 134, **134**, 147, 148, **148**, 149, 151, 152, **152**, 153, **153**, 154, **154**, 155, 156, **156**, 157, 158, **159**, 160, **160**, 161, **161**, 162, **163**, 165, 166, **166**, 167, 169, 170, 172, **174**, 175, 176, 177, 179, **179**, **180**, 181, **181**, 182, **182**, 185, 187. *See also* ghost; "Wonder of the Seas"

Great Lakes, 14

Great Western Railway, 147

Greenland, 107, 130

Greenwich, England, 154

Guayaquil, Ecuador, 50

Guilford, Connecticut, 31, 33

Gulf of St. Lawrence, 55, 175

Gulf states, 39, 140

gutta percha, 78, **78**, 81, 96

Gutta Percha Company, 78, 96, 148

H

"Hail Columbia," 117

Halifax, Nova Scotia, 59

"Hallelujah," 123

Hamilton, Alexander, 25

Handel, G. F., 123

Harper's Weekly, **116**, 119

Hartford, Connecticut, 31, 111

Heart's Content, Newfoundland, 149, 151, 162, 166, 167, 172, 173, 174, 175, 176, 177, 180, 182, **182**, 183, **183**, 185

Henry, Joseph, 123

Hoboken, New Jersey, 36

Holland, 60

Housatonic River, 13, 32

Housatonic Valley, 17

House of Commons, 147

"How Cyrus Laid the Cable," 8, 119

Hudson River, 14, 19, 21, 22, 28, 29, 36, 38, 187

Hunt, Wilson, **58**

Huntington, Daniel, **58**

I

Ice Glen, **14**

Iceland, 130

Illinois, 80, 133

India, 129, 132

International Cable Jubilee, 120

Ireland, 56, 60, 77, 79, 82, 83, 84, 85, 86, 98, 103, 107, 109, 114, 119, 122, 125, 127, 129, 157, 159, 160, 162, 164, 166, 167, 171, 172, 175, 179, 181, **182**. *See also* Foilhummerum Bay; Lord Lieutenant of Ireland, Earl of Carlisle; Queenstown; Skellig Islands; Valentia; Valentia Bay; Valentia Island

Irish Sea, 75

Isthmus of Panama, 50, **50**

J

James Adger, 65, 66–71, **70**

James River, 139

Jamestown Island, 139

Johnson, Andrew, 176

Judson, Isabella Field (daughter), 42, **44**, 187. *See also* Field, Isabella

junk dealer, **34**, 35, 131

Justice, 117

K

Kentucky, 53

L

Labrador, 59, 130, 185. *See also* Newfoundland and Labrador

Lee, Massachusetts, **28**, 29

Leopard, 82, 90

Lima, Peru, **44**

Lincoln, Abraham, 133, **133**, 135, 137, 138, **139**, 140, 141, 142, 143, 144, **144**, 146, 151; death of, 155

Liverpool, 38, 81, 83, 84. *See also* Associated Press, Liverpool

Liverpool Stock Exchange, 76

London, 11, 39, **40**, 72, 75, 77, 78, 81, 83, 90, 99, 103, 129, 134, 142, 143, 144, 145, 147, 167

London Stock Exchange, 112

Longfellow, Henry Wadsworth, 111

Long Island, 36

Lord Clarendon, 75

Lord Lieutenant of Ireland, Earl of Carlisle, 86–87

M

Madison Avenue, 39

Madison Square Presbyterian Church, 135

Magdalena River, 45, 46

Maiden Lane, New York City, 32

Maine, 9, 59, 72. *See also* Portland

Manhattan, 25, 26, **27**, 33, **36**, 37, 39

Marcos, 48, 50

Maryland, 140. *See also* Antietam; Baltimore

Massachusetts, 14, 21, **28**, 119. *See also* Berkshires; Boston; Housatonic River; Housatonic Valley; Ice Glen; Lee; Stockbridge; Westfield

Massachusetts regiment, 138

Maury, Matthew, Lieutenant, 57

McClellan, George, 139

Mediterranean Sea, 60, 82

Medway, 172, 175, 176, 177, 178, 179, **179**

Mercantile Library, 26

Merchants' Exchange, 25–26, **27**

Metropolitan Hotel, 125, 185

Michigan, 21, **24**, 26

Midwest, 72, 95

mirror galvanometer, **96**, 97, 127, 158

Montgomery, Alabama, 137

Morse, Samuel F. B., 57, **58**, 65, 66, **66**, 74, 75, 77, 84

Morse code, 65, **66**, 77, 97

International Morse Code, **66**

Mullaly, John, 65, 67, 71, 84, 88–90, 99, 105, 106, 107

Muzo, New Granada, 47

N

Narrows, New York Harbor, 117

Narrows, St. John's, Newfoundland, 67

New Brunswick, 9, 72, 111. *See also* St. John

New England, 32, 53, 66

Newfoundland, 9–11, 53–56, **56**, 59, 61, 63–65, **64**, 67–68, **69**, 72, 79, 80, 82, 85, 86, 90, 95, 106, 107, 114, 119, 128, 129, 130, 148, 156, **160**, 164, 165, 167, 170, 174, 181, **182**, 183, **183**, 185

attorney general of, 59

bishop of, 112
Executive Council, 113
governor of, 59, 118
Legislative Council, 118
legislature, 10, 79.
    See also Bull's Arm; Cape Ray; Heart's
    Content; Narrows, St. John's,
    Newfoundland; Newfoundland and
    Labrador; Port-aux-Basques; St.
    John's; Trinity Bay
Newfoundland and Labrador, 185
Newfoundland dogs, 67, 68, 71, 156
New Granada (now Colombia), 45. *See
    also* Barranquilla; Bogotá; Bogotá
    River; Magdalena River; Muzo; Puracé
    volcano; Savanilla; Tequendama Falls
New Haven, Connecticut, 26, 37
New Jersey. *See* Cape May; Hoboken
New Orleans, 23, 43
New York. *See* New York City; New York
    State
New York, Newfoundland and London
    Telegraph Company, **58**, 59, 60, **64**, 75,
    113, 130, 135
    directors, 59, 60, 71, 130
New York City, 9, 10, **10**, 11, 19, 21, 22–26,
    22, **27**, 28, 29, 32, 33, **34**, 35, **36**, 37, **38**,
    39, 40, **40**, 50, **50**, 53, **54**, 55, 56, 57, 59,
    71, 72, 76, 79, 82, 91, 99, 106, 108, 113,
    114, 115, 117, 119, 120, 122, **123**, **124**, 128,
    128, 129, 130, 131, 133, **133**, 134, **134**,
    135, 138, 142, 143, 145, **146**, 147, 155, 181,
    182, 187
    archbishop, 112, 120
    mayor, 120
    post office, 25.

    See also Astor House hotel; Battery;
    Battery Park; Broadway; Brooklyn
    Navy Yard; Burling Slip; Central
    Park; Chamber of Commerce; City
    Hall; City Hall Park; Coney Island;
    Croton Aqueduct/Reservoir; Crystal
    Palace; draft riot; East Twenty-first
    St.; Gramercy Park; Madison Avenue;
    Madison Square Presbyterian
    Church; Maiden Lane; Manhattan;
    Mercantile Library; Merchants'
    Exchange; Metropolitan Hotel; Pier
    4; post office; Printing House Square;
    Seventeenth St.; Sixth Avenue; St.
    Patrick's Cathedral; Staten Island;
    Third Avenue; Tiffany's; Trinity
    Church; Union Square; Wall Street
New-York Commercial Advertiser, 133
New York Daily Tribune, **128**
New York Harbor, 45, 57, 117. *See also*
    Narrows, New York Harbor; Statue of
    Liberty
New York Herald, 65, 84, 90, 108, 110, 112
New York State, 21, 39. *See also* Albany;
    Buffalo; Castle Garden; Erie Canal;
    Hudson River; Seventh Regiment;
    Seward, William, as New York senator
New-York Times, **128**, 131, 145, 167
Niagara, **80**, 81, 82, 83, **82–83**, 84, 85, **85**,
    86, 87, **88**, 90, 97, 98, **98**, 99–103, 104,
    106–108, 112, 113, 114, 116, 117–118, **118**,
    120, **121**, 122, 127, 148, 152, 157
Night-Watch, The, 163
North America, 9, 21, 54, 55, 60, 61, 107, 111,
    118, 158, 170, 184
North Atlantic Ocean, 56, 91, 98
Nova Scotia, 9, 55, 56, 59, 66, 68, 72. *See
    also* Cape Breton Island; Cape Sable
    Island; Halifax; Sydney

O

"old coffee-mill," 87, 103
O'Neil, Henry, 162, 163

P

Pacific Ocean, 50, 140
Panama, 50. *See also* Aspinwall; Isthmus of Panama
Paris, 76
Parliament, 170
peace conference, 137
Pender, John, 147, 170
Pennsylvania. *See* Gettysburg; Philadelphia
Peru, 49. *See also* Lima
Philadelphia, 26, 33, 112
Pier 4, 65
Pierce, Franklin, 79, 81
Pilgrim's Progress, The, 19, 27
Plymouth, England, 91, 97, 98, 99, 101
poop deck, 87
Porcupine, 107, 156
Port-aux-Basques, Newfoundland, 66, 67, 68
Portland, Maine, 111, 167
Printing House Square, **128**
Propontis, 71
Puracé volcano, New Granada, 49

Q

Queenstown, Ireland [now Cobh], 84, 102
Quito, Ecuador, 48, 49

R

Red Sea, 132
rendezvous point, mid-Atlantic Ocean, 99, 100, 101, 102, 103, 104

Revenue Act, 138
Revolutionary War, 13, 79
Rhine River, 38
Roberts, Marshall, 58, **58**
Russell, William, 156, 162, 164, 166
Russia, 170. *See also* St. Petersburg
Russian America, 146, 185, 186. *See also* Alaska
Rutland, Vermont, 112

S

sabotage, 162, **163**
San Francisco, 140, 146
San Jacinto, 141, **141**
Santiago, Chile, **44**
Sarah L. Bryant, 61, 65, 66–71, **70**
Savanilla, New Granada, 45
Saxe, John Godfrey, 8
Scotland, 76, 130
Seventeenth Street, New York City, 36, 38
Seventh Regiment, New York state, 138
Seward, William: as New York senator, 79, 133; as U.S. Secretary of State, 139, 142, 155
sextant, 106, 164, 177
Shaffner, Taliaferro, 95, 130
Sheerness, 152, 154, **154**, 156, 172
shore-end cable, 82, 86, **86**, 87, 108, **109**, 154, 157, 158, **158**, 166, 172, 173, **173**, 175, 183
Siberia, 146, 167
Singapore, 78
Sixth Avenue, 123
Skellig Islands, 157
slavery, 133, 143
Smith, Willoughby, 171
Smithsonian Institution, 123
South, 33, 138, 142. *See also* Confederacy

South America, 23, 41, 43, 44, **44**, 45, 48, **49**, 51, **51**, 53. *See also* Chile; Ecuador; New Granada; Peru

South Carolina, 135, 137. *See also* Charleston Harbor; Fort Sumter

Sphinx, 153, 161, 165, 167

St. John, New Brunswick, 111

St. John's, Newfoundland, 10, 55, 59, 67, 72, 79, 90, 108, 113, 114, 165, 175

St. John's Daily News, 167

St. Patrick's Cathedral, 119

St. Petersburg, Russia, 146

Staten Island, 117

Statue of Liberty, 187

Stewart, Mr. A. T., 22, 24, 25, 27, 28, 35

Stockbridge, Massachusetts, 13, 14, **14**, 18, **24**, 28, 29, 45, 48, 49, 51, **51**, 53, 114, 139, 187

Stone, Joseph
business partner of, 33, 37, 40–41, 53
death of, 60
marriage, 40

Stone, Mary Elizabeth Field (sister), 60, 75
death of, 76
marriage, 40.
See also Field, Mary Elizabeth

Susquehanna, 81, 82, 98

Sydney, Nova Scotia, 71

T

Taylor, Moses, 58, **58**

Telegraph Construction and Maintenance Company, 148

Telegraphic Journal, 147

telegraph lines in U.S., 9, 37, 39, 54, 55, 57, 95, 140, 146

telegraph station, Ireland, Foilhummerum Bay, Valentia Island, 157, 159, 162, 171, 172, 173, **173**, 174, **176**, 180

telegraph station, Ireland, Valentia, 84, 85, 87, 89, 108, 109, 127

telegraph station, Newfoundland, Bull's Arm, Trinity Bay, 90, 104, 106, 107, 108, **109**, 112, 113, 119, 127, 128, 156

telegraph station, Newfoundland, Cape Ray, 68, 69

telegraph station, Newfoundland, Heart's Content, 176, **183**, 185

Tennessee, 53

Terrible, 153, 165, 166, 172, 173, 177

Tequendama Falls, 48

Thames River, 77, 152, 154, **154**, 166

Third Avenue, New York City, 36

Thomson, William, 76, 77, 81, 84, 96, **96**, 97, 99, 102, 127, 130, 132, 156, 158, 171

Tiffany's, 119

Times, 127, 142, 156

Tomás, 48

Trent, 141, **141**

Trinity Bay, Newfoundland, 90, 104, 106, 107, 108, 112, 114, 125, 128, 129, 149, 157

Trinity Church, **36**, 120

Turkey, 15

U

"Uncle Judge," 140

Union, 138, 141, 142, 143, **144**, 145, 155
assistant secretary of war, 138
military, 135, 138

Union Square, New York City, 116, 123

United States, 10, 13, 21, 26, 37, 38, 44, 48, 54, 55, 57, 61, 72, 76, 77, 79, 81, 86, 90, 91, 98, 108, 111, 114, 115, 120, 131, 133, **133**, 137, 141, **141**, 142, 147, 153, 155, 167, 172, 175, 176, 182, 185, 186
Congress, 79, 80
House of Representatives, 79, 80
Senate, 79, 80, 133.

See also East Coast; Gulf states; Midwest; New England; Union; West

United States Naval Observatory, 57

U.S. ambassador to Great Britain. *See* Adams, Charles

U.S. Marines, 26

U.S. Navy, 15, 79, 81, 82, 84, 95, 151; Navy secretary, 151

U.S. Secretary of State. *See* Steward, William

V

Valentia, 86, **86**, 87, 89, 108, 109, 115, 122, 129, 162, 172, 174, **176**, 180, 181, **181**

Valentia Bay, 166

Valentia Island, 86, 107, 157, 173. *See also* Foilhummerum Bay

Valorous, 98

Victoria, 63, **64**, 68, **70**, 71, 90

Victoria, Queen, 108, 112, **113**, 114, 115, 119, 125, 129, 138, 155, 175, 176, **176**, 185

Virgil, 19

Viva, 45

W

Wall Street, 25, 187

War Department, 138, 139; telegraph office, 138

War of 1812, 13, 79

Washington, D.C., 31, 57, 79, 80, 95, 137, 138, 139, 140, 142, 151, 175. *See also* peace conference; Smithsonian Institution; War Department; White House

Washington, George, 13, 123

West, Stephen, Dr., 13

West (U.S.), 33, 91

Western Union, 72, 140, 146, 147, 167, 170

Westfield, Massachusetts, 32

West Indies, 98

Whig party, 27

White, Chandler, **58**, 59

White House, 138

Whitehouse, Edward, Dr., 76, 77, 81, 84, 85, 89, 97, 99, 109, 114, 127, 130

William Cory, 172, 173

Williams College, 15, 19, 29

Williams, Cyrus, 13

"Wonder of the Seas, The" 135, 147, 151

world's fair, 39, **40**, 120

Y

"Yankee Doodle," 119

PICTURE CREDITS

Courtesy of **Atlantic-Cable.com Website**: Jacket (back), 10, 61, 69, 70, 78, 80, 82–83, 84, 85, 86, 88, 96, 98, 100, 101, 109, 157, 158, 159, 174, 183.

The Berkshire Eagle: archives, 51; August 2, 1858, 123.

Charles Bright, ***The Story of the Atlantic Cable***: 56, 153.

Chapin Library, Williams College, gift of members of the Field family: 24.

Cooper Hewitt, Smithsonian Design Museum/Art Resource, NY: gift of Louis P. Church, #1917-4-120: 49.

Mary Morton Cowan: 64; from cover of *Harper's Weekly*, September 11, 1858: 121.

Timothy M. Cowan: 160, 179.

Courtesy of **Donald Drack**: 46.

Frank Leslie's Popular Monthly, August 1886: 16.

Granger, image #0038646: 38.

Provided courtesy **HarpWeek**: ID #6EC74287W8141342Y: 116; ID#7DF40044FJ872761U: 122.

Illustrated London News: August 15, 1863: 146; August 5, 1865: 176.

Isabella Field Judson, ***Cyrus W. Field: His Life and Work***: 18, 44, 163.

Library of Congress, Prints and Photographs Division: LC-D4-72605: 14; LC-USZC2-3141: 35; LC-USZC4-2106: 36; LC-USZC4-5040: 118; LC-USZ62-7725-A: 133; LC-USZ62-111072, Detail: 139; LC-B8171-2351: 140; LC-B8171-7929: 144.

Copyright © Metropolitan Museum of Art/Art Resource, NY: Painting by William James Bennett, bequest of Edward W. C. Arnold, #54.90.130: 22; Eight paintings by Robert Charles Dudley, gift of Cyrus W. Field: #92.10.68: 105; #92.10.75: 152; #92.10.55: 154; #92.10.76: 156; #92.10.67: 161; #92.10.69: 166; #92.10.44: 173; #92.10.43: 181.

Museum of the City of New York: Charles D. Fredericks & Co, F2012.58.486: 32.

National Portrait Gallery, Smithsonian Institution/Art Resource, NY: NPG.80.213: 186.

Photography © New-York Historical Society: Map of the City of New-York. Cyrus W. Field & Co., Paper Warehouse, No. 11 Cliff Street, New-York. Paper of any size and weight made to order at short notice . . ., ink on paper, M7.5.26, inventory no. 2613, image # 87229d. Detail: 34.

The New York Public Library, Digital Collections: 1650770: 27; ps_prn_848: 128.

Courtesy of **Panama Tourism & Travel**: 50.

Historical Collection, Stockbridge, MA, Library: 15, 58, 182.

ThoughtCo.com, The Trent Affair: 141.

Courtesy of **Special Collections, University of Houston Libraries**. Detail: 54.

Wikimedia Commons©: CyrusField4.jpg, photo by Napoleon Sarony: front jacket (top) and 6; Columbia_Mills,_Lee,_MA.jpg, from a postcard: 28; New_York_Crystal_Palace.jpg, oil color plate by George Baxter: 40; International_Morse_Code.svg, chart by Snodgrass and Camp, 1922: 66; Queen_Victoria_-_Winterhalter_1859.jpg, Royal Collection RCIN 405131, reproduction of a portrait by Franz Xaver Winterhalter: 113; CyrusField3.jpg, photo by Mathew Brady: 124; SS_Great_Eastern_in_New_York_Harbor_by_Stacy.jpg, from an 1860 stereogram: 134; Great_Eastern_painting_smooth_sea-2.jpg, lithograph by Charles Parson: 148.

Wünschendorff, E. *Traité de Télégraphie Sous-Marine*, Librairie Polytechnique, Paris, France, 1888: front jacket (bottom) and 178 (reversed from original), 180.